Table

SHADOWS IN THE ATTIC

An Unfinished History of Horror

J.F. GONZALEZ

Published by Apokrupha Books
Cover by Lynne Hansen

Introduction

Growing up in the 1970s/1980s, there was no world wide web, so horror fiction fans who wanted to dive deeper into the genre had to use sources other than the internet to look up things. Stephen King's Danse Macabre was required reading, as were the non-fiction of and lists compiled by Karl Edward Wagner (appearing everywhere from back issues of The Twilight Zone magazine to his Introductions in the annual Year's Best Horror anthologies). Fanzines were also a cornucopia of knowledge and facts, but the inherent problem with zines was their slapshot availability. H.P. Lovecraft's Supernatural Horror In Literature was another great resource, but—at the time—suffered from the same scarcity as many of the zines.

Young J.F. (Jesus) Gonzalez memorized all of these and more. Living in Southern California, he had somewhat easier access to those zines than those of us living in flyover country did, via availability at cool underground comix shops and alternative bookstores. Perhaps more importantly, he had access to the still-living horror writers of legend, as well. A truth not many fans know about—when he was barely out of college, Jesus would often drive the legendary Robert Bloch to the grocery store and help him with his shopping. Indeed, among Jesus's papers (soon to be part of a university collection) was one of Robert Bloch's shopping lists.

Right now, some of you might be saying "Who was Robert Bloch?"

And if you are one of those people, then you are who Jesus was writing this for.

(Robert Bloch was a mentee of H.P. Lovecraft, and a mentor of authors you probably do know, including Stephen King, F. Paul Wilson, Jack Ketchum, John Skipp, and David J. Schow—who, in turn, have been mentors to writers such as Jesus and myself. Bloch is most famously known as the author of Psycho, but that is just a drop in his very large bucket of contributions to the genre).

Most of the material in this book originally appeared as columns in Lamplight magazine, I vividly remember how excited Jesus was when he signed with editor and publisher Jacob Haddon to do this. Both of us had known Jacob for years, and we both had an immense amount of respect for him and belief in him, so we knew Jesus would be in good hands. And this was stuff Jesus desperately wanted to write about—the history of horror fiction, particularly the areas that don't get talked about often, or indeed, at all. Jesus loved talking about this stuff. As years went by, and we got older and grayer, he began to grow weary of the convention and book signing circuit, particularly the months-long marathon promotional tours we used to do. But that weariness would vanish any time a fan or reader asked him a question about some obscure writer, or ghost stories from the medieval era done as woodcuts, or a long-forgotten pulp magazine. He knew about them all, and he spoke about them all with the exuberant zeal of a true fan. Jesus was never known in academic circles, but he knew more about the horror genre than most of the academics who make their living knowing about it. And indeed, those few academics who did know Jesus would often come to him for help with their research.

When Jesus died, his family lost a husband, father, and son. I lost my best friend. Horror fiction fans lost one of the best, most dependable writers of our generation. But the genre itself? The genre lost a veritable fountain of knowledge. Yes, unlike when Jesus and I were young, we do now have the world wide web, and all of the knowledge in the world is available at our fingertips. Or so we like to tell ourselves. The truth is, it isn't. There are always facts that fall through the cracks. Human history is rife with forgotten peoples and locations and events and dates. Horror fiction is the same way. There are many now-forgotten authors and publishers and magazines and stories. But Jesus remembered them all and had read them all. And sadly, that source of knowledge is irreplaceable.

But we do have these columns—and though Jesus never lived long enough to see this series to complete fruition—we've included some other essays by him (from other venues) that are in the same vein. If you want to know more about the genre's history, this is a great place to start. And if you think you know all that there is to know about the genre's history, then you're about to be proven wrong.

Anyway... I'm going to shut up now, and let my friend have fun talking about stuff that he loved one last time.

Brian Keene, somewhere along the Susquehanna River
June 2022

SHADOWS
IN THE
ATTIC

An Unfinished
History of Horror

Why History 101 is Fundamental

W hile I was at the last Horrorfind Convention in August, I had an interesting and brief conversation with a budding writer at a dealer's table. We made light and pleasant banter about the kind of topics that generally amuse those of the creative bent until the writer seized the opportunity to go on a self-promotion kick. In addition to the 200 stories the writer had seen published in the past two years in everything from *Bloody Skulls Webzine* to *Rotting Zombies* magazine, said writer had been interviewed no less than twenty times in similar publications. Impressive to a degree, and while I had never heard of the writer in question I didn't let on to this fact. If it made him happy to be published in such obscurity, who was I to begrudge the fact? Obviously he loved writing and being published, and as much as I tried to be polite when he asked me if I had ever heard of the publications he had appeared in, I'm afraid I disappointed him with my continued responses of "No, I've never heard of that magazine/webzine/anthology, etc." Finally, in an attempt to steer the conversation into something other than the writer's own work and perhaps toward a common ground, I noticed an advertisement for Night Shades Publications' *Gods in Darkness* by Karl Edward Wagner. "Cool!

Somebody is finally collecting Karl's Kane novels. Can't wait for this to come out."

The hotshot writer I was conversing with looked confused. "Who's Karl Edward Wagner?"

I turned to him. "You're kidding, right?"

A shake of the head. There really was confusion in those muddled eyes.

"*In a Lonely Place?*"

Still a blank stare.

"Ever read 'Sticks'?"

Another shake of the head.

Okay, fine, I thought. Maybe he's never come across Karl's work. It could happen. "'Sticks' is still in print," I offered. "Its in *The Dark Descent*, edited by David G. Hartwell, and you can pick it up anywhere. It's got great stuff in it."

"Who else is in it?"

I started listing the writers and stories that I knew were in that essential volume, at least those I could remember off the top of my head. The writer nodded at the mention of Stephen King and Clive Barker and H. P. Lovecraft, but drew that confused look again when I mentioned other names: Shirley Jackson, Nathaniel Hawthorne, Edith Wharton, Russell Kirk, Harlan Ellison, Robert Bloch. I decided to try a little test. "Hell, it's got 'Yours Truly, Jack the Ripper' by Robert Bloch in it."

"Robert Bloch..." The writer's voice was a questioning whisper, as if by enunciating the word he could somehow conjure the memory of where he might have come across that byline.

"Yeah, Robert Bloch. You know... *Psycho?*"

"Oh yeah!" Recognition flooded his features. He was on familiar ground.

Perhaps the previous evening's company had spoiled me. I had spent most of it in a sports bar off the hotel with John Pelan talking about writers like Bob Leman, Jane Rice and others who produced wonderful work but had fallen into relative obscurity, a topic John and I, as well as half a dozen other people I know of, can talk about for hours on end. It's also inevitable that whenever I hang out with other writers, conversation turns toward the work of those we admire, usually writers who are not just familiar by name, but held in high regard by fans of the genre unless they're quite obscure.

But to not know who Karl Edward Wagner is?

Or Robert Bloch?

I asked the hotshot writer who he generally reads and he ran off a list of the three big names in our field, as well as writers like Jack Ketchum and Edward Lee. Fine talent, all of them, and writers I enjoy myself. He also proceeded to list dozens of new writers, many of them recognizable to me, as well as other writers who, again, I've never heard of. "Who's George Hotshot Writer again and where can I find his work?" I asked in response to hearing a name I'd never heard of.

"Oh George is great! He's had about fifteen hundred stories published in a lot of really gushy places like *Worm Holes in Your Flesh* magazine and—"

"That's great, and I'm sure your friend appreciates your support but, um... you ever heard of David Schow?"

"David who?"

I'm afraid I've since forgotten the name of the chap I was talking to, but the point I want to illustrate is this: ignorance of the work of those that have come before you can be hazardous to your career as a writer.

Unfortunately, there is a small yet growing number of writers who have arrived on the horror scene of late who have had a recent epiphany after reading a few Stephen King novels which deludes them into thinking they can do this, too; many of them don't even bother to soak up the classics of the field. Those who have been involved in the field for the past ten years or more, as I have, will probably argue that there have always been such well-intentioned but misguided people. This is true. The difference between then and now is that it is much easier for them to be published due to the web and self-publishing POD outfits like Xlibris (mediums which can be both a blessing and a curse) than it ever has been. No, I won't single out any writers in this piece, and bear in mind that I say a *small* group, not all of them, tend to remain ignorant of who folks like Theodore Sturgeon are. (In discussing this phenomena with friends, I've actually heard anecdotes in which other self-proclaimed 'hotshot writers' have never read the work of writers whose work is readily available in mass market like, say, Bentley Little, for the simple reason that their work doesn't appear on Internet Publications, which is what these people confine their reading to). There's a lot of new writers out there who are talented, smart, and who *do* read widely—they're not whom I aim this essay at.

Rather, my comments are directed toward those who have no idea who Robert Bloch, Karl Edward Wagner, David Schow or—God forbid—Charles Beaumont might be.

To become an Applications Programmer it takes a degree of skill, knowledge, and training to do the job; one must have a background in computer science, and have a working—if not proficient knowledge—of various computer programming languages and platforms. Likewise, to be a veterinarian takes dedication, discipline, and an education that is akin to obtaining a Medical Degree. Likewise, once one gets into medical school they decide on a specialty—cardiology, psychiatry, gastroenterology, pediatrics, among others. Should you develop a heart condition you would want to entrust your care to the best cardiologist available, would you not? Of course! Likewise, should you break your leg you wouldn't trust your care to your cardiologist, would you? (unless you have a heart attack after breaking your leg, but I digress).

Wouldn't it stand to reason, then, that if you wish to write compelling, memorable, rich dark fantasy/horror fiction that you read as widely as possible in your chosen genre? And that you are aware of the rich traditions of our field and be familiar with some of the many classic short stories, novellas, and novels produced prior to, say 1990?

Keeping up to date with current work is fine, and supporting your friends and peers is admirable. But if you limit your reading to 'what is current', or the work of your friends, the small press, webzines like *Bloody Skulls On the Web* (before any of you start typing that in a search engine, I'm being sarcastic; to my knowledge there is no such webzine as *Bloody Skulls*, but there are dozens of webzines out there like it), you're doing yourself, and your writing, a disservice. To illustrate another analogy, a teenager getting interested in playing the drums might be initially inspired by drummers of the hot current bands now, but what drummers were those musicians influenced by? And what musicians were *those* drummers influenced by? How far back can you trace the influential lineage?

Stephen King may be the most widely read author of horror fiction in history, but he'll be the first to admit that he was influenced by writers like Richard Matheson, Robert Bloch, and Ray Bradbury.

And Robert Bloch was influenced by H. P. Lovecraft.

Lovecraft was greatly influenced by Poe, Dunsany, and—

Get the picture?

And it's not just horror fiction a burgeoning writer should be reading, either. To be a good writer period, one should read as widely and as much as possible, both fiction and non. Melville, Dickens, Faulkner, Hemingway, Hardy, Tolkien, Silverberg, Hammett, Chandler, Thompson... well, the list goes on. Limiting yourself to a few big names in our field like King or Anne Rice and the current small press stuff will shut out a wealth of material that was published before you discovered the field.

Knowing what's been done before is important.

Knowing how to take an old theme and find a new twist or slant on it is even better.

Coming up with your own voice and creating tales that are fresh and original is even harder. Those that do are writers who have a firm grasp on what's been done before. They're steeped in the history of literature; not only in their chosen genre, but in literature in general.

I'll be the first to admit that it's impossible to read everything that's been published before, and to limit your reading strictly to 'the classics'... but you *should* be intimately familiar with most of the classics in our field, and in literature in general, if you want to produce work that is rich in theme, metaphor, plot, imagery, and language.

So where to start?

If you haven't read the classics since they were forced on you in high school, dig them up, make trips to used bookstores and buy a couple. Read them. Read anthologies, paying special attention to reprint anthologies of classic horror fiction. If you see reference to a work in an anthology or some other source that strikes your interest, hunt it down. Keep doing that, following the links as you go. Definitely continue to pursue your other reading interests. Don't have time to read? If the book you're currently reading now is a paperback, take it with you wherever you go. You'll be surprised by how many pages you can get in while waiting in line at the grocery store.

Keep doing this while continuing to write (and spend more time writing and reading fiction and less time writing on internet message boards) and in a few years you'll be well-read, you'll have learned what's been done before, and you won't look at me cross-eyed if I ask you what you think of M.R. James or John Farris.

I might be able to forgive you if you give me a blank stare if I rave about Eddy C. Bertin, Clive Pemberton or Jean Ray.

But I'll have to smack you if you ask me who Fritz Leiber is.

Reprint Anthologies

The first installment of this column is coming under an extreme deadline. Originally intended to shine a light on lesser-known authors (and books) newer writers should seek out and read, I still plan to do that. However, because of the tight deadline, we're going to start off with something a little different.

But first, a brief introduction of sorts. One of the things that sparked the idea for this series of articles was noticing the looks of befuddlement new writers and fans of the genre give me whenever I casually mention a writer like Karl Edward Wagner or Charles L. Grant. A quick probing of their reading interests usually elicits the following: they came to the field by way of Stephen King and Dean Koontz, of course, and also Clive Barker and perhaps Peter Straub. Some of them might pick up one of the latest Year's Best compendiums like Paula Guran's *The Year's Best Dark Fantasy and Horror* or Ellen Datlow's *Year's Best Horror*. Some might even pick up Lovecraft because they've heard good things about him. What they all have in common: they keep up with the current state of the field.

This is all fine and good. Quite a lot of them, however, never bother to dip back in the not-too-distant history of this genre. Part of the problem might be that NY Publishers simply aren't issuing reprint anthologies like they used to and these newer writers miss them.

When I was a young fan of the genre, much of my education of the deep history of fantasy, horror, and science fiction came from reprint anthologies.

The first was *Ten Tales Calculated To Give You Shudders,* a 1972 anthology my mother bought me when I was around ten years old. This volume (edited by Ross R. Olney from Golden Press and clearly geared toward the youth market of the mid-seventies) was my first introduction to "adult" horror fiction—Robert Bloch, William Hope Hodgson, Frank Belknap Long, H. Russell Wakefield, and other writers of the pulp era (the lone exception being a Robert G. Anderson tale culled from the pages of *Alfred Hitchcock's Mystery Magazine* from 1966). Prior to that, I'd been reading books geared towards kids my age, usually purchased from the Scholastic Book club. And comic books. I was heavily into DC and Marvel's horror titles, especially *Man-Thing, Werewolf by Night, Weird War Stories, House of Secrets,* and *House of Dracula.*

That anthology was my first taste of serious horror fiction. When I began to take a more serious interest in this type of fiction, the so-called "horror boom" in publishing was in full swing. It was a terrific time to be a fan of this genre: there were so many quality anthologies being published at that time, all of them featuring the works of the then contemporary writers of the day (Charles L. Grant, Stephen King, Harlan Ellison, etc), and reprinting the classic tales from decades past (Bloch, Bradbury, Wellman, Matheson, etc). Anthologists like Charles Grant and Stuart David Schiff combined original fiction with reprints in many of their anthologies. You could find dozens of reprint volumes in the large chain bookstores of the day (B. Dalton's Books or Waldenbooks) and second-hand bookstores by the likes of August Dereleth, Mary Danby, Robert Aickman, Richard Dalby, and Peter Haining. Marty Greenburg and Robert Weinberg (often in collaboration with other editors) were beginning to issue volumes reprinting tales from the pulps and the Edwardian/Victorian era. And for the yearly roundup of what was happening currently, there was Karl Edward Wagner's *The Year's Best Horror Stories.*

In short, reprint anthologies were the textbooks for my education in the field.

The good news is reprint anthologies are still being published. Nightshades Books and Prime Books are doing an excellent job in issuing reprint anthologies on a wide range of themes and styles. Penguin Classics issued S. T. Joshi's *American Supernatural Tales* a few years ago. In 2009 Library of America published Peter Straub's *American Fantastic Tales: From Poe to the Pulps* and *American Fantastic Tales: Terror and the Uncanny from the 1940's to Now* (both are also available as a boxed set). Running Press and Carrol & Graf publish the reprint anthologies Stephen Jones puts together. You should try as many of these anthologies as you can. You might not like every story, but you will probably find quite a bit of material you will like by acknowledged masters of the genre.

You'll also learn a bit of the genre's history, too.

And that's a good thing.

Reprint anthologies, more than any other, I believe, do more to preserve the history of the genre than original anthologies or magazines. While many reprint anthologies are built around a theme (genre tropes like Vampires, Ghosts, Zombies) or adhere to a specific time period (Victorian era, the pulp era, etc), there are some that I feel can be considered text books for those who wish to immerse themselves in a complete education of the history of supernatural/weird fiction. What follows are my recommendations on five reprint anthologies I feel fit these criteria. All five feature some story overlap, but all are worth seeking out for the material the editors of these volumes ferreted out and for the rich, informative introductory essays that preface each volume.

And for the pure geek factor: there was so much cool stuff published before a lot of you were born.

Great Tales of Terror and the Supernatural, edited by Herbert A. Wise and Phyllis Fraser first appeared in 1944 from Random House. It's been reprinted numerous times since its first appearance, and the edition I have is the 1994 Modern Library edition, that I believe is still in print and still available. Going as far back as 1832 to reprint "La Grande Breteche" by the great French writer Honore de Balzac, this volume served as the benchmark for other anthologists. Reprinting classic, often-reprinted tales by the likes of Poe, H. G. Wells, William Faulkner, Ambrose Bierce, and M. R. James, this volume also reprinted then-contemporary tales like "The Sailor-Boy's Tale" by Isak Dinesan and Carl Stephenson's "Leningrad Versus the Ants." The list of authors and stories is simply nothing short of incredible: Algernon Blackwood, E. F. Benson, A. E. Coppard, Ambrose Bierce, Saki, Edith Wharton, Rudyard Kipling, Charles Dickens, Nathaniel Hawthorne, H. P. Lovecraft, even Ernest Hemingway! The tales run the spectrum from the classic English ghost story, to the early weird fiction of Edward Lucas White, to the gothic, cosmic horror of Lovecraft (then a new thing for the mass audience who might have happened upon this volume in their local Pickwick or Barnes and Noble). In short, a volume every serious devotee of horror fiction should not only own, but read.

Equally important is David G. Hartwell's wonderful *The Dark Descent*. Containing fifty-six stories and novellas, most of the material contained in this volume should be familiar with long-time readers of the field. Editor David G. Hartwell prefaces each piece with a short critical essay. His introduction traces the history of horror and supernatural fiction and its place in literature and is required reading for any serious student of the field. Sharing space with the familiar tales (Fritz Leiber's "Smoke Ghost" and Robert Bloch's "Yours Truly, Jack the Ripper") are obscure gems like the creepy 1882 tale by Lucy Clifford "The New Mother" to works of classic literature ("The Lottery" by Shirley Jackson; "Good Country People" by Flannery O'Conner). Every sub-genre is included: the gothic (Edgar Allan Poe's "The Fall of the House of Usher"; Science-Fiction ("The Autopsy" by Michael Shea); Lovecraftian ("The Call of Cthulhu" by Lovecraft, "Crouch End" by Stephen King, and "Sticks" by Karl Edward Wagner), and the quiet ("If Damon Comes" by Charles L. Grant).

Hartwell followed up *The Dark Descent* with a companion volume in 1992—*The Foundations of Fear*. This volume focuses more on the novella or short novel length rather than the short story. As a result, you have familiar tales like Richard Matheson's classic "Duel" and "At the Mountains of Madness" by H. P. Lovecraft, but you also have tales like "The Entrance" by Gerald Durrell, one of the strongest tales of gothic horror involving mirrors I've ever encountered. Hartwell goes even further back in time than Wise & Frazer with "The Sandman," an 1819 novella by E. T. A. Hoffman (which still holds up today nearly two hundred years later). Like *The Dark Descent*, the tales run the gamut from the psychological to the Science-Fictional, to offerings from writers of classic English Literature ("Barbara, of the House of Grebe" by Thomas Hardy) to pure modern horror fiction ("In the Hills, the Cities" by Clive Barker). *The Foundations of Fear* was my first introduction to the work of Belgian weird-fiction writer Jean Ray, represented here with "The Shadowy Street".

Alas, both the Hartwell volumes are out of print, but are well worth tracking down through used book dealers, or on Amazon or Ebay.

Two recent anthologies to this list are currently in print and easily available. *The Century's Best Horror Fiction* edited by John Pelan (CD Publications) and *The Weird: A Compendium of Strange and Dark Stories* edited by Ann and Jeff VanderMeer (Tor Books). The editors of both anthologies present their selections in chronological order, which is something geeks like me love. The Pelan volume presents one story from each year of the twentieth century he found as "the best". There are some excellent choices here, some obvious standards that were no-brainers, and a few minor quibbles (as much as I love "The Tower of Moab" by L. A. Lewis, I would have gone with "The Three Marked Pennies" by Mary Elizabeth Counselman for the 1934 entry, but that's just me). Starting with the 1901 entry ("The Undying Thing" by Barry Pain... a wise choice), Pelan includes familiar often-reprinted classics and rare outstanding tales even I'd never encountered before ("The Lover's Ordeal" by R. Murray Gilchrist). It was nice to see Ulric Daubeny's "The Sumach" represented in this volume (one of the most under appreciated tales of vampirism I've ever encountered). This two-volume set represents all forms and styles—ghost stories, science-fictional horrors, psychological horror, the conte cruel, contemporary supernatural horror, surreal. All in all, this is a very worthy entry, but it comes with a hefty price tag. A two volume hardcover set, this will set you back $150. If you can afford it, this will be money well spent.

A more affordable solution (with more stories!) is the VanderMeer volume. Published as an attractive trade paperback from Tor Books, at over 1,000 pages it is a doorstopper of a book (this title is also available as an eBook, and I believe there is a trade hardcover as well)! As of this writing I have barely waded in to it. Despite that, I heartily recommend it. What sets this volume apart from the others is this is an anthology focusing on weird fiction; therefore, all forms of weird fiction are included—the surreal, the decadent, the Gothic, Lovecraftian, etc. Weird fiction can be beautiful, it can be strange, it can be unsettling. As a result, the stories included here are all over the map. Not only does this anthology contain many classics (and a lot of my personal favorites!), the editors also found wonderful material from the early pulp years (like the excellent "The People of the Pit" by A. Merritt and "Unseen—Unfeared" by Francis Stevens) and they include an array of tales by writers around the world with new English translations (as a long-time fan of Jean Ray, I am especially pleased to see two of his tales reprinted herein). The rare pulp entries (the aforementioned Merritt and Stevens pieces, as well as rare gems like "The Night Wire" by H. F.

Arnold and "Mimic" by Donald A. Wollheim) and the translated entries are proving to be the real winning points for me. I've never encountered Luigi Ugolini's "The Vegetable Man," nor Ryunosuke Akutagawa's "The Hell Screen" before; both are utterly absorbing. As of this writing, I have only gotten as far as Robert Barbor Johnson's "Far Below" (an excellent choice)... which means I am barely a quarter of the way through. Despite that, I can't recommend this anthology enough. The Table of Contents features some very familiar tales and names (Jerome Bixby's classic "It's a Good Life!," "Sandkings" by George R. R. Martin, Stephen King's "The Man in the Black Suit") to tales that are completely unfamiliar to me ("The Other Side of the Mountain" by Michel Bernanos). This anthology is really that good and deserves a place on your bookshelf.

(Peter Straub's two-volume *American Fantastic Tales* should probably be mentioned here too as being volumes you should look into acquiring. A quick perusal of the Table of Contents indicates some excellent choices: stories by Charles Brockden Brown, who authored *Wieland, or The Transformation* in 1798—probably the first Gothic novel published in the U.S—as well as tales by W. C. Morrow, Charlotte Perkins-Gilman, F. Scott Fitzgerald, August Derleth, Jack Snow, T. E. D. Klein, Thomas Tessier and dozens of others).

I would consider these anthologies to be the ultimate textbooks for having a solid grounding in the field of imaginative, dark, weird fiction.

The beauty of reprint anthologies, especially those that dig deep within the genre's history, is they will often feature works by writers one may have missed entirely. This was the certainly the case for me in first coming across the work of

Jean Ray, Eddy C. Bertin, David Case, or Charles Birkin (who I encountered in an anthology edited by Marty Greenberg). These days I own collections of short fiction by most of these guys (and I wish some enterprising U.S. publisher will issue a collection of Eddy C. Bertin's horror fiction in English translation). I would never have come across any of their work if it hadn't been their appearance in various reprint anthologies.

So. There is your list to start you off. Go forth and purchase these volumes. Read them. If you like the work of a particular author, research them to find out what else they may have written. Repeat and rinse as necessary. I'll be back next time to ruminate on the works of a few neglected authors from decades past. Until then, happy reading!

The Year's Best Horror Stories

L ast installment I made a brief mention of my informal education of the rich history of dark fantasy and horror fiction. One of the titles I mentioned was Karl Edward Wagner's *The Year's Best Horror Stories*, which was a yearly anthology series published by DAW books in mass-market paperback.

DAW's *The Year's Best Horror Stories* series was important for many reasons (and the Wagner-edited volumes are so important, they were listed in Stephen Jones and Kim Newman's *Horror: Another 100 Best Books* in the Recommended Reading List section). I'll get to that in a moment. But first, let's do a roundup of annual Year's Best anthologies most of you are probably familiar with.

There are currently three annual Year's Best Compendiums that do a fine job of culling through dozens, if not hundreds, of magazines, web 'zines, anthologies, and other venues to present you what their editors have deemed 'the best' in today's contemporary horror and dark fiction. Of course, your mileage may vary from story to story, but I heartily recommend all of the following anthologies anyway. The editors involved are seasoned professionals, and they know a good story when they see it. And in one case (Ellen Datlow's *Best Horror of the Year*), there is an Honorable Mentions List for stories that didn't make it in that year's volume but are worth seeking out.

Best Horror of the Year (Night Shade Books), edited by Ellen Datlow—Now in its fourth year, this annual series replaces Datlow's (with co-editors Terri Windling, Kelly Link & Gavin Grant) previous *The Year's Best Fantasy and Horror* (St. Martin's Griffin), which ran for over twenty years. Datlow does an admirable job in compiling a good selection of stories from a number of sources, and she keeps the mix well-rounded. You'll find traditional ghost stories, tales of psychological horror, slipstream, and all manner of dark fiction. It is an excellent showcase of the best in dark fiction.

Best New Horror (Running Press) edited by Stephen Jones—An annual mainstay since its debut in 1990, Jones' series probably comes closest to replacing Wagner's *The Year's Best Horror Stories*. You really can't go wrong with this series. While I have heard some complain that *Best New Horror* is heavily tilted in favor of British writers, I find these complaints without merit—a good story is a good story, no matter the country of origin of the writer. Jones manages to reprint worthy (and superior) work by writers who were once mainstays in the field who have since been forgotten by more modern readers. Case in point: in the latest volume (Volume 23), a posthumous story by Evangeline Walton that was published last year in F&SF. Walton is the author of a classic novel in the field—*Witch House*, which Arkham House published in 1945. Jones' broad background and knowledge in the field, and his appreciation for the history of classic horror is a much-needed asset in today's publishing climate.

The Year's Best Dark Fantasy and Horror, edited by Paula Guran (Prime Books)—A relatively new arrival on the scene, this is a thick annual volume that covers horror and dark fantasy and is well worth your purchase. Guran presents stories the other two editors might not include in their yearly compendiums for the simple fact that they fall more within the dark fantasy genre, which a lot of horror fans may miss. A good example of this is "A Haunted House of Her Own" by Kelley Armstrong from the debut volume, a writer more known for her novels of Dark Fantasy and Paranormal Romance.

Year's Best anthologies are not really that new. These annual showcases have been around in one form or another since 1949 (with Everett F. Bleiler and T. E. Dikty's *The Best Science Fiction Stories*). One could argue that a prototype for these types of showcases for horror and science fiction was the *Not at Night* series, which were published in England from 1926 to 1936 and edited by Christine Campbell Thomson. While Thomson included some original material, most of the stories from the early volumes were reprints from U.S. pulps like *Weird Tales*. Thomson's selections during this period can be seen as a literal Best Horror of the Year for this time period, with such authors as August Dereleth, Frank Belknap Long, H. P. Lovecraft, Robert E. Howard, and Seabury Quinn appearing in its pages. Those were the writers who were the cream of the crop in the field in the late 1920's and early 1930s.

Macabre tales were often included in the various Year's Best SF anthologies that appeared throughout the 1950's and 1960's. Long-running series like *The Pan Book of Horror, The Fontana Book of Great Ghost Stories* and *The Fontana Book of Great Horror Stories* included excellent reprints, often going back to the Victorian and Edwardian era; for example,

Edward Lucas White's "Lukundoo"—from 1907 and reprinted in this issue of *LampLight*—was included in one of the *Pan Book of Horror* volumes. The majority of these volumes comprised of original stories, which doesn't really make them Year's Best series *per se*, but they come close in that they were an annual mainstay. It wasn't until 1971 that an annual Year's Best series was devoted *entirely* to the horror tale.

The Year's Best Horror Stories was launched by Sphere Books in England, with Richard Davis as editor. Three volumes appeared between 1971–1973, with DAW books reprinting the first volume (and cherry-picking tales from the Sphere Volume 2–3 for their US reprint of Volume 2). By the time DAW took over the series in the United States with Volume 3, Davis was gone and replaced by Gerald Pearce as editor.

Pearce and Davis were capable editors, but the series really didn't hit its stride until Karl Edward Wagner took over with Volume 8. Wagner edited the series until his untimely death in 1994.

I discovered the series with Volume 8 and faithfully bought and devoured each new edition when it hit the stands. Later, I found used copies of previous volumes (including the Sphere editions) at second-hand bookstores. Readers who like a good hunt through used bookshops or who don't mind searching online, and would like a sample of what was current back in horror fiction's glory days of the 1980's should seek this series out.

One thing that set the Davis and Pearce-edited volumes from Wagner's was the first seven installments often featured an average of two original stories per volume (the exception was the very first volume, which was entirely comprised of reprints). The official reason for this was that the editors often couldn't find 60,000 words of worthy material to reprint. I imagine it might have been a somewhat difficult task to ferret out enough quality material in the 1970's to fill each volume. However, a quick perusal of a private list I maintain of quality material published during that time period shows Davis and Pearce really didn't have to hit up writers for original stories had they expanded their search to include low-grade men's magazines and the small press magazines of that era. Curiously missing from the first seven volumes are such classics as Karl Edward Wagner's own "Sticks," Stephen King's "The Mangler" and "Gray Matter," Ramsey Campbell's "The Companion," Joyce Carol Oates' "Nightside," among dozens of other tales by the likes of Bill Pronzini, David Case, Richard Laymon, and Janet Fox. Then again, word limits imposed by DAW were probably a factor as well.

Whatever the case, despite those minor quibbles, the Davis and Pearce volumes are worth seeking out. The first volume reprints "Prey" by Richard Matheson and other excellent material by the likes of E. C. Tubb, Kit Reed, David A. Riley, and Eddy C. Bertin. Volume 2 (of the DAW Series) reprints "The Events at Poroth's Farm" by T.E.D. Klein, and "The Animal Fair" by Robert Bloch, a story I still think about whenever I see a real-life carnival. Subsequent volumes reprint tales by Brian Lumley, Harlan Ellison, Ramsey Campbell, David Campton, and others. Some of the original stories that appeared in the Pearce-edited volumes have become classics in their own right: "If Damon Comes" by Charles L. Grant, and "Drawing In" by Ramsey Campbell would have been deemed worthy for inclusion for reprinting in a Year's Best volume had they appeared elsewhere first. They're that good.

What made the Wagner-edited incarnation of *The Year's Best Horror Stories* so special? Lots of reasons, primarily Wagner's encyclopedic knowledge of the rich history of the field, coupled with his own sensibilities as a writer. Wagner not only reprinted excellent material by the older masters of the time (Hugh B. Cave, Robert Bloch, Manly Wade Wellman), he also featured works by well-known writers who were at the top of their game and at the height of popularity for that era (Stephen King, Ramsey Campbell, Charles L. Grant). Newbie writers like David J. Schow, Elizabeth Hand and Wayne Allen Sallee were always welcome. Some of the newbie writers would never publish another story ever again. Others continue to work in the field today. Wagner's sources were far-reaching and wide—literary journals, mainstream magazines like *MayFair* and *Playboy*, chapbooks, UK small press magazines like *Kadath*, newsstand genre publications like *F&SF*, *Rod Serling's The Twilight Zone Magazine*, and *Asimov's*, to small press horror magazines like *Whispers* and *The Horrorshow*, to anthologies like *Shadows*—one story was culled from *Outlaw Biker Tattoo* magazine!

Wagner cast his net far and wide. One of his major coups was reprinting the title story from Terry Lamsley's debut (and self-published) collection of regional ghost stories, *Under the Crust*. Wagner found the book in a gift shop in England and brought it to the attention of other editors and the World Fantasy Convention, where the title novella copped the award for best novella the following year. Today, Lamsley is one of the most respected writers of the weird tale.

Throughout the 1980's, *The Year's Best Horror Stories* was *the* yearly Year's Best anthology for horror fiction—it was the *only* one until Datlow and Windling's *The Year's Best Fantasy and Horror* appeared in 1988 (the first two volumes were under the title *The Year's Best Fantasy*—horror fiction was always included in the series). Stephen Jones's *Best New Horror* made its debut in 1990 (with Ramsey Campbell as co-editor for the first five volumes). There was a brief appearance of what I'd hoped would be another contender—*Quick Chills: The Year's Best Horror From the Small Press* from Deadline Press. That series only lasted two volumes. (In 2006 there was another hopeful: *Horror: The Best of the Year*, edited by Sean Wallace and John Betancourt from Prime Books. Unfortunately, no further volumes were printed despite cover mock-ups appearing on Amazon.com and writers reporting they'd had stories slated for appearance).

During his tenure as editor of *The Year's Best Horror Stories*, Wagner featured tales of quiet horror, psychological suspense, ghostly tales (the best of these were of the M. R. Jamesian type, reprinted from the now defunct *Ghosts & Scholars* magazine), surreal horror, splatterpunk, and out-and-out contemporary horror in the Stephen King mode. He also wasn't afraid to be experimental—he continually reprinted the works of Wayne Allen Sallee, then horror's reigning king of the small press scene, as well as the work of mad poet t. Winter-Damon.

Starting around 1990, Wagner's selections became more eclectic. While keeping to the series roots, Wagner began to feature more experimental work, and continually began to rely more on the small press. A quick comparison of the Jones/Campbell and Datlow/Windling volumes shows the most overlap. Compared to *The Year's Best Horror Stories*, there was hardly any overlap, and Wagner would include material originally published in markets so obscure, even *I'd* never heard of them. Therefore, it wasn't surprising that Wagner would be the first to reprint the works of David Niall Wilson, Yvonne Navarro, or Terry Lamsley.

Sadly, *The Year's Best Horror Stories* died with Wagner, who succumbed to an embolism brought on by long-term alcoholism on October 14, 1994. Upon Wagner's passing, DAW Books decided to cancel the series, which was probably for the best. The series had become so identified with Karl that a replacement would simply not have worked.

In perusing the Wagner-edited run of *The Year's Best Horror Stories*, some of the same bylines appear in almost every volume (in the case of Ramsey Campbell, two entries in the same volume). Some writers appear for a few years, then drop out of sight. Far more common are those writers who only had one appearance in this seminal series—these writers range from masters like Richard Laymon (who appeared in Volume 10 with a nasty piece of work called "The Grab") to writers who published a handful of excellent tales in their brief careers and vanished from the scene— "The Devil Behind You" by Richard Moore in Volume 8, and "Cruising" by Donald Tyson are really good examples of this. Just as common are writers who are still active in the field today, who might not be as visible as the current flavors-of-the-month, but are still producing excellent work; Lawrence C. Connolly is a perfect example... he appeared in two volumes of *The Year's Best Horror Stories* in the early 1980's with tales that still stick with me—"Echoes" and "Mrs. Halfbooger's Basement". Another example is Al Sarrantonio, who first made an impression with me with his early stories "Pumpkin Head" and "The Man With Legs".

Of course, what's more fascinating is watching the rise of what was then a new writer on the scene. David J. Schow was a relative unknown when he made his debut in *The Year's Best Horror Stories* in 1984 (with "One For the Horrors"), as was Simon Clark who appeared two years later with "...Beside the Seaside, Beside the Sea." Elizabeth Hand appeared in the series in 1989 with her very first published story (from *Rod Serling's The Twilight Zone Magazine*). Nowadays, Clark, Hand, and Schow are household names, and you should all be reading them.

In addition to the fiction, Wagner often provided a brief listing of the then-current magazines—both small and professional—and anthologies that published horror fiction in his introduction to each volume. Reading these now is like viewing a time capsule, one I wish I could go back to at times. For those of you who weren't there when it was all happening, these introductions, and more importantly the stories themselves, will entertain and frighten you. A lot of them will leave a lasting imprint on you.

For those who like your books in hardcover, a good portion of the Wagner-edited volumes (and the last Pearce-edited volume) were reprinted by Underwood-Miller under the title *HorrorStory*. Three thick volumes appeared between 1989 and 1992, each one reprinting three of the *The Year's Best Horror Stories*. The original plan was to reprint the entire series (including the Sphere volumes) in hardcover, but Underwood-Miller dissolved shortly after the third volume of *HorrorStory* appeared.

So. If you have the time and the patience, seek out the Wagner-edited *The Year's Best Horror Stories*. Copies can be found abundantly online—try *abebooks.com*. In addition, seek out the older Pearce and Davis edited volumes as well. The entire series is well worth the time and the effort to seek out and read (and if you're as big a geek as I am about this stuff, start with the first volume and work your way forward). You'll be glad you did.

On *The Horror Show*

This installment was originally intended to be Part Two from our last outing ("From the Stone Age to the Early Victorian Era, in 3,000 words"). As the sub-title suggests, in that installment I attempted to provide a very rough history of the development of horror fiction as a way to segue to some future topics I have planned. Because it is virtually impossible to provide even a Cliff-Notes version of the entire history and development of a literary genre, I provided only scant highlights and, even then, I had space issues, hence the two-parter. This installment was originally intended to be Part Two.

Unfortunately, the field has lost three influential writers back in March (2013), all within a seven day period, which necessitated a change of plans for this installment.

While two of those writers were very well-known to aficionados of horror and dark fiction, the third influenced the field in a way that is not readily apparent unless one takes the time to do some digging.

The writers in question? Two of the more well-known, James Herbert and Rick Hautala, passed within one day of each other (March 20 and 21 respectively). James Herbert was a best-selling author in his native England. He hit the scene with a splash in 1974 with his novel, *The Rats*, a grisly tale of mutant rats that overrun modern day London. *The Rats* was the precurser to what became known as the British Nasties, the U.K.'s equavalent of the splatterpunk sub-genre. The story was gory, the violence gruesome for its times, and the sexual situations very bold for 1974. Herbert followed up this first effort with several entertaining and influential novels including *The Fog, Moon,* and two sequels to *The Rats—Lair* and *Shrine.* Several of his novels were adapted to film. Not all of his work can be placed in the hardcore horror category, but some of his early work was certainly a forerunner, and laid the groundwork for what was to come.

Rick Hautala passed away unexpectedly the following day from a heart-attack. Hauta emerged on the scene with his 1981 novel *Moondeath.* His 1986 novel *Night Stone* was one of the first to feature a holographic cover, a design that helped propel the book onto the bestseller lists. While primarily a novelist, Hautala also turned to the short form from time to time as evidenced by his 2000 collection *Bedbugs.* Hautala's specialty was the ghost story, and several of his novels demonstrated his story-telling talent. His powerful prose and finely crafted, chilling tales lingered with you long after you turned the last page. A recipient of the 2012 Horror Writer's Association Life Achievement award, Hautala was a regular at Necon and other regional genre conventions. He was a congenial and happy-go-lucky guy, always quick with a smile and a joke, or words of advice if you asked him. I feel fortunate enough to have known him and I will miss him.

Almost a week before the unfortunate passing of both these fine writers and gentleman, though, was that of David B. Silva, who died quietly at his home in Las Vegas, Nevada, probably around March 11 or 12 (the news of his death was first reported on March 14, but Silva had apparently passed a few days before that). Most new readers of the field might recognize him as the former editor and publisher of *Hellnotes*, the web magazine he co-founded (with Paul F. Olson) and ran (until he sold it to Journalstone late last year). Some may even know him from his short fiction and his more recent books (*The Shadows of Kingston Mills* or *Through Shattered Glass*); if this is the case, then you know Silva was a masteful writer, and I consider several of his tales to be classics ("Dwindling," "The Calling" "Brothers," "Dry Whiskey," among others). You might even be aware that he was the publisher/editor of *The Horror Show* back in the 1980's.

To convey just how influential *The Horror Show* was is a somewhat difficult task. So many readers who are new to the field (those who discovered it post 9/11) may have *heard* of *The Horror Show*, but few of them have seen it, nor do they understand how influential it was. To communicate how David Silva's magazine helped shape modern horror fiction is something I will attempt to explain in this installment.

To put it bluntly, *The Horror Show* was a huge influence on Richard T. Chizmar's seminal magazine *Cemetery Dance*. Without *The Horror Show*, there probably would be no *Cemetery Dance*. And without *The Horror Show*, the careers of writers like Poppy Z. Brite, Brian Hodge, Elizabeth Massie, and Bentley Little might have turned out very differently; I dare say, in some cases, they might not have happened at all.

The Horror Show was certainly not the first small press magazine devoted to contemporary horror fiction (that honor probably goes to *Macabre*, which was launched by Joseph Payne Brennan in 1957). The field of SF/Horror has always had amateur publications. H. P. Lovecraft got his start writing for various amateur presses, even publishing one himself (*The Conservative* from 1915–1923). The amateur presses of the early twentieth century were self-published magazines and journals devoted to all manner of topics, mostly publishing essays and articles, along with fiction and poetry.

As science-fiction fandom began to take shape in the 1930's, fans began to publish their own magazines. Influenced by the pulp magazines of the day, they launched such titles as *The Fantasy Fan, Unusual Stories,* and others. While crudely made (usually run off stencils or mimeographs and stapled together), they attracted original work by the leading names of the day and published the earliest writings of authors who went on to bigger and better things—Robert Bloch's first published story, "Lilies" (1934) appeared in *The Fantasy Fan* a full six months before his first professionally published story that launched his career in *Weird Tales* ("The Feast in the Abbey," January 1935)

Throughout much of the 1930's and into the 1970s, these amateur magazines ranged in production quality from simple mimeographed publications (with text set on a typewriter) to professionally typeset and printed efforts. They were primarily distributed and sold at science-fiction conventions and by mail order. Occasionally, bookstores that dealt primarily in science-fiction and fantasy would stock them.

The 1970's saw several important titles that were several steps above the old-fashioned mimeograph fanzines: *Weirdbook, Fantasy Tales,* and *Whispers.* Primarily influenced by the classic *Weird Tales* pulp, these magazines, while still considered fanzines due to the fact they didn't have newsstand distribution and did not pay their contributors professional rates, were much more than that. While the layout and typography of the early issues of all three of these magazines was, at times, crude, they were lovingly put together, and featured the leading talents the field had to offer in prose and art. The quality of material published within their pages was very high. The problem was their frequency of publication. Many were bi-annual. If you were lucky, you could get three issues a year; sometimes, though, you only got one. Sometimes an entire year or two would pass before a new issue would arrive.

Of course, there were other small press horror magazines in the 1970's and early 1980's as well (*Eldritch Tales, Space & Time, Moonbroth*), but like the above mentioned titles, their owners/editors ran these publications more as a hobby than as an actual enterprise. Mail order or attending a genre convention was probably the only place you'd be likely to stumble on one.

David B. Silva's magazine *The Horror Show* changed all that. While the first issue (November 1982) wasn't much to look at, it improved with the next few issue. By the end of 1983 it had gone from being printed on newsprint (and looking more like a small newsletter) to a standard magazine size with a two-color cover and plain white paper for the interiors. It wasn't a top-notch glossy professional publication by any means, but it had heart. It had attitude. And by this time, familiar genre stalwarts like Janet Fox and J. N. Williamson (then a paperback novelist who was churning out horror novels for such houses as Zebra and Leisure) were contributing original fiction to its pages.

Prior to all this, there hadn't been a steady horror fiction magazine published in the United States since *Weird Tales* folded its doors in 1954. While SF magazines like *Fantastic* and *The Magazine of Fantasy and Science Fiction* often featured horror fiction within their pages, their primary focus was on science-fiction and fantasy, not horror. Other digest-sized magazines that managed to survive the implosion of the pulp era occasionally published contemporary horror fiction. Most of these were the mystery digests like *Mike Shayne's Mystery Magazine, Alfred Hitchcock's Mystery Magazine,* and *Ellery Queen's Mystery Magazine*. For a time in the 1960's and early 1970's, Health Knowledge, Inc. in New York published a series of digest-sized pulps largely comprised of reprints from earlier titles like *Weird Tales* or *Strange Tales*. Occasionally they'd publish new, original material by genre favorites like Joseph Paynne Brennan or newbies like Stephen King and F. Paul Wilson (the magazines in question were *Startling Mystery Stories* and *The Magazine of Horror*). For the most part, though, there wasn't a consistent magazine that published contemporary horror fiction with national newsstand distribution that paid professional rates to writers.

So when *Rod Serling's The Twilight Zone Magazine* hit the stands in early 1981, it became the first horror magazine in almost thirty years to have national newsstand distribution. Started by Montcalm Publications, it started as a monthly, switching to bi-monthly in 1982. It paid top rates for fiction and, as a result, the genre's leading writers appeared in its pages: Harlan Ellison, Stephen King, Robert Bloch, Peter Straub, as well as writers just starting out at the time—Joe R. Lansdale, David J. Schow, John Skipp, and dozens more. While much of its content centered around the seminal television series it was named after, it also featured articles, reviews, and fiction with a *Twilight Zone* bent. By late 1984, Montcalm had added a sister publication to TZ—

the digest-sized *Night Cry,* which focused entirely on contemporary horror fiction.

(As an aside, *Weird Tales* had been revived three times by 1984; neither incarnation lasted beyond a few issues, and newsstand distribution was so spotty it hardly counts to even mention it here).

The Horror Show was launched at a time when Stephen King's popularity was exploding and *Rod Serling's The Twilight Zone Magazine* was hitting its stride. The horror boom in publishing was just getting underway. It seemed that horror fiction was becoming increasingly popular.

By the time I discovered the *The Horror Show* with its Summer 1984 issue, TZ was the only newsstand periodical that consistently published horror fiction. Seeing *The Horror Show* on a genuine magazine rack, at a B. Dalton's Bookstore, was something I'd never seen before. How Silva managed to get his little magazine this kind of distribution, I haven't a clue. For the first few years of its existence, most of his contributors were beginners or small press veterans, but it wasn't long before he his little magazine began to attract the work of more professional writers: Joe R. Lansdale, Ramsey Campbell, David J. Schow, and Richard Christian Matheson all contributed fine, original fiction to its pages during this period. The new writers Silva published, while not known outside the realm of the small press, were becoming familiar to me: Bentley Little, Elizabeth Massie, Kevin J. Anderson, Poppy Z. Brite, Paul F. Olson, A. R. Morlan, Brian Hodge. The features and interviews grew; the artwork improved. And by mid 1986, the production changed—gone was the thick-coated cover stock that had been used for the covers, replaced now by a more standard four-color glossy stock that is now common with genre publications. The interior paper stock changed too. The typesetting was now done with better computer equipment. And along with the change of production values saw the first major contribution by Dean Koontz, who appeared in the Summer 1986 issue with two original stories and an interview.

Over the next three years, *The Horror Show* would go on to publish the work of Dennis Etchison, Gary L. Raisor, Donald R. Burleson, Thomas F. Monteleone, Al Sarrantonio and other talents. It became the genre publication to submit fiction to. Other genre publications at the time—*Rod Serling's The Twilight Zone Magazine* and the revived *Weird Tales*—paid better and ran excellent fiction, but there was something about *The Horror Show* that was special. The fiction David Silva published in its pages was original, and at times daring and unique. *The Horror Show* was a showcase for contemporary horror fiction the way *Weird Tales* was a showcase for contemporary horror and weird fiction in the 1930's.

Every issue contained original fiction by new and up-coming talents and well-known writers, interviews with authors and filmmakers, book and movie reviews, and story illustrations. Joe R. Lansdale wrote a column on horror fiction in prose and film (mostly focusing on B-movies) called "Lansdale's House of Horrors". In the magazine's later years, Thomas F. Monteleone's long-running M.A.F.I.A column appeared within its pages. One of the more unique features in the magazine was a recurring column called "Fragments of Horror" that featured extracts from a specific writer's notebook of story ideas. Some of these were excerpts of novels-in-progress that were never published (*Gore Movie* by David J. Schow and *They Still Thirst* by Robert R. McCammon).

Much of the excerpts, though, were a few sentences per entry—story ideas, character studies. Some of the more fascinating and memorable ones were from the notebooks of William F. Nolan, Richard Christian Matheson, J. N. Williamson, and Ramsey Campbell.

By the mid and late 1980's, *The Horror Show*'s influence was felt throughout the little small-press community. Other publications sprang up, some of them very good (*Grue Magazine, New Blood, 2AM Magazine, Deathrealm, After Hours, Cemetery Dance*). Many of them were obviously aping The Horror Show's look and feel. One of the things Silva did early on was publish a *Rising Stars* issue, featuring five writers and one artist he considered an up-and-coming talent within the genre. Each writer contributed two original stories and was interviewed for the issue; the artist was also interviewed and had a special portfolio of their work. The first *Rising Stars* issue (Fall 1987) featured Poppy Z. Brite, Bentley Little, Elizabeth Massie, A. R. Morlan, and G. Wayne Miller, plus an art portfolio by Allen K. A second *Rising Stars* issue was published two years later (Summer 1989) and featured Paul F. Olson, Gary L. Raisor, Brian Hodge, and Susan M. Watkins. I've never seen a small-press editor/publisher focus an entire issue of their magazine on writers who were still testing their wings and developing their chops, but Silva recognized talent when he saw it.

(I think Silva was the first to start the trend of having special issues, where a good chunk of the issue is devoted to a specific writer. Robert McCammon and Dean Koontz each had two, and Silva also had special issues devoted to William F. Nolan, John Skipp & Craig Spector, and Dennis Etchison.)

Citing a need to return to his first love—writing—Silva announced the magazine's demise in the Spring of 1989 and produced the final issue a year later. By the time that issue came out (Spring 1990), the magazine had launched the careers of Brian Hodge, Bentley Little, Elizabeth Massie, A. R. Morlan, Poppy Z. Brite, Gary L. Raisor, and Paul F. Olsen and had published a total of twenty-nine issues. These writers went on to great things in the years that followed. Many of the magazines that were inspired by Dave's work with *The Horror Show* continued on. One of those magazines—*Cemetery Dance*—continues on to this day. Others that didn't last as long left their own marks in the field.

It's possible that without *The Horror Show*, such talented writers as Poppy Z. Brite, Brian Hodge, Elizabeth Massie would not have had a venue that exposed them to a hardcore readership that would come to clamor for their work. Early readers and fans of their work were avid readers of *The Horror Show*—I was one of them. Poppy Z. Brite's first novel, *Lost Souls*, might not have been written had her short story "A Taste of Blood and Altars" not appeared in the Summer 1988 issue. This story provided the seed for *Lost Souls*. The same can be said for Brian Hodge's career as a novelist; his first published short story, "Oasis," became the basis for the first novel he sold (*Oasis*, Tor Books, 1989). Joe R. Lansdale published some of his early work in the pages of *The Horror Show* (two of those stories, "The Shaggy House" and "The Fat Man" became linked to his Lord of the Razor universe). One of his most infamous works of all time is his short-short "My Dead Dog, Bobby," which originally appeared in the Summer 1987 issue.

In addition to exposing the work of the aforementioned writers to a wider audience, *The Horror Show* influenced the field in another way: it demonstrated that others could produce a periodical just as good, on a similar budget. Starting around 1986, dozens of horror small press publications were started by enterprising publishers. Most were pale imitators to *The Horror Show*, but a few went on to great things: *Deathrealm* and *Cemetery Dance* come to mind. In the late 1980's and throughout the 1990s, beginning writers could learn their chops in these little magazines. There are fewer small press horror magazines these days, but those that are around today owe their existence to *The Horror Show*.

Readers who want to sample the kind of fiction David Silva published in the pages of *The Horror Show* are encouraged to seek out his anthology *The Definitive Best of The Horror Show* (CD Publications, 1993, and out of print). This is an expansion of an earlier volume published by 2AM Publications in 1987 (*The Best of The Horror Show*). The CD version contains all the stories in the original 2AM edition and adds over a dozen more. The stories range from tales by writers who would only appear a few times in the magazine ("Wolf is Waiting" by Mark A. Parks) to writers who seemed to appear in every issue (Bentley Little is represented with two of his stories—"Witch Woman" and "Runt"). It features little-known works by genre masters ("The Mystery Buff" by David J. Schow and "Self-Possessed" by Steve Rasnic Tem) and works that should be considered classics by now (the aforementioned "The Shaggy House" by Joe R. Lansdale and "The Scar" by Dennis Etchison). Despite such a stellar line-up, with good material, a follow-up volume is sorely needed to reprint stories that are just as good, that probably couldn't be worked into this volume due to space issues—"Company" by John Skipp and Craig Spector, "14 Garden Grove" by Pierre Comtois, "Phallasies" by Brian Hodge are just a sampling of the tales I'd include in a follow-up volume if given the chance to put one together.

Until (and if) that happens, I direct you to Amazon.com or Abebooks.com to buy the CD trade hardcover of *The Definitive Best of The Horror Show*. Ebay is a good resource for tracking down back issues of *The Horror Show*, but be wary—the average price on most back issues is around $10–15 each, with older issues fetching much higher prices.

From the Stone Age to the Early Victorian Era, in 3,000 Words

Scary stories (i.e., horror fiction, dark fantasy, supernatural fiction, etc) have been around forever, but there were no bona-fide "horror writers" (i.e., writers who wrote nothing *but* horror fiction) until the so-called horror "boom" in publishing during the 1980's. Of course, many writers wrote horror fiction for the pulps and their successors, the digest magazines, throughout much of the 20th century, and a slew of others flirted with the form during the Edwardian and Victorian era (as well as the years preceding). For many of these writers, horror was just one of many genres they wrote in. But when they wrote what we know as horror, they did it well.

(And it should be noted that in those Edwardian and Victorian times, the term "horror-fiction" was rarely used to describe tales of terror—*ghost story* and *gothic fiction* were the usual terms.)

As HPL wrote in his landmark essay "Supernatural Horror in Literature" (1924–1934) "The oldest and strongest emotion of mankind is fear, and the oldest and strongest kind of fear is fear of the unknown." It's pretty likely that the first storyteller's around prehistoric campfires were tales of horror and the unknown; oral story-telling in this fashion no doubt provided the perfect outlet to explore early man's own fears of what was Out There (Saber-toothed tigers that killed and ate you, of course). Fictional stories also explored early man's developing spiritual awareness and superstitions.

Therefore, it shouldn't come as a surprise that some of the earliest stories ever committed to parchment were epic tales that included scenes of horror and the supernatural: "Theseus and the Minotaur" from 1500 B.C., being a prime example (and let's not forget the Greek epics "The Iliad" and "The Odyssey"). One of the earliest surviving manuscripts of Old English literature, *Beowulf* (circa 700-1000 A.D.), is abound with horrific imagery and supernatural themes. Other examples include *The Oresteia* (458 B.C.) by Aeschylus and, of course, that old standby from Dante Alighieri—*Inferno* (itself the first part of his epic poem *Divine Comedy*).

Poets and playwrights during the Elizabethan era certainly used horrific imagery—witness *The Tragedy of Macbeth* by William Shakespeare, *The White Devil* by John Webster, *The Tragical History of Doctor Faustus* by Christopher Marlowe, and *The Revenger's Tragedy* by Cyril Tourneur. These plays can certainly be classified as some of the earliest examples of horror fiction, even if pretentious Literature professors at major universities say otherwise. While recognizing that terror was a part of the human condition, these playwrights exploited the emotion of terror and fear in their plays to great extent and to great acclaim from their audiences. And while these works have gone on to be deemed great works of literature by academia, during their heyday many of these plays were written with future academic canonization the furthest thing from the collective minds of their creators—they were written primarily to entertain the audience (and, in some cases, royalty), and to express personal opinions on contemporary topics of the day.

William Shakespeare, probably the greatest of all the Elizabethan playwrights, was immensely popular with the masses and, on occasion, mauled by the critics. His plays frequently dealt with a wide-range of human emotions—love, rage, revenge, jealousy, murder, regicide (back then an extremely serious offense), madness, and religious hysteria. Quite often, Shakespeare's plays dealt with the supernatural—witness the witches in *Macbeth*, or the ghosts in *Hamlet*.

Despite all these great examples, these were not the first stories written primarily to scare its readers.

While the gothic novel is often thought of as the jumping point of the birth of horror fiction, the aforementioned plays and epic poems certainly laid the groundwork. Shortly after the reign of the Elizabethan-era playwrights and poets, the novel as a literary form was born. Most novels published during this period were realistic, both in respect to contemporary times and history, and in their tone. That all changed with the publication of what is arguably the first gothic novel (and the first horror novel), *The Castle of Otranto* by Horace Walpole, in 1764.

Prior to that, the work of Daniel Defoe (1660–1731) is often overlooked by many scholars as having a place in the development of the gothic and what we come to know as modern horror fiction. Defoe is probably most famous for his adventure/thriller novel *Robinson Crusoe* (1719). While not a horror novel in the conventional sense, *Robinson Crusoe* was the first novel published in the English language, was a huge influence on writers who came after him, and certainly paved the way for the gothic influence. Jonathan Swift's 1726 novel *Gulliver's Travels* was certainly influenced by Defoe's novel (and *Gulliver's Travels* is awash in supernatural imagery). In addition to *Robinson Crusoe*, Defoe authored several short stories, two of which can be seen as early precursors to horror—"The Magician" (1726) and "The Ghost in All the Rooms" (1727).

Despite this, the work of Defoe and Swift were primarily realistic in tone, and were more rooted in adventure. In today's marketplace, they would be classified as thrillers.

That all changed with Walpole's *The Castle of Otranto*. While it reads rather goofy by today's standards, in 1764 *The Castle of Otranto* was very popular with readers in Georgian England and ushered in the genre of gothic fiction. Between 1776 and 1820, hundreds of novels were published utilizing Walpole's motifs—a mystery that was often threatening to the main character, an ancestral curse, and countless trappings such as hidden passages in crumbling, decaying ancestral estates. There was often a sense of the supernatural or superstitious elements, and an evil villain. Many were poor retreads of Walpole's novel and (later), retreads of *The Monk* (1796) by Matthew Gregory Lewis. Some of the better early gothics of this period include *Vathek* by William Beckford (1786), *The Mysteries of Udolpho* by Ann Radcliffe (1794), *The Midnight Bell* by Francis Lathom (1798), and the *Old English Baron* by Clara Reeve (1778). Some of the more amusing titles (by virtue of their title, not their actual plotlines) included *The Animated Skeleton* by Anonymous (1798), *The Necromancer; or, The Tale of the Black Forest* by Lorenz Flammenberg (1794), *The Witch of Ravensworth* by

George Brewer (1807), *The Demon of Sicily* by Edward Montague (1807), and my favorite (in terms of the title... not the actual novel): *Manfrone; or, The One Handed Monk* by Mary Anne Radliffe (1809).

(As an aside, it should be noted that many gothics were originally published anonymously. The most famous of these was *Frankenstein, or The Modern Prometheus*, in 1818; Mary Wollstonecraft Shelly did not add her byline to the novel until its 1822 reprint, which was only issued following the success of a stage play based on the novel that had been produced the year prior.).

The gothics were formulaic, to be sure, and their basic framework would be utilized one hundred and forty years later in the 1930's in the U.S. "shudder-pulp" or "weird-menace" pulps. To wit: much of the narrative thrust of the gothic was filled with supernatural events, with evil villains that threatened the virtue of a virginal maiden, yet at the end the supernatural events were explained away, often revealed to be elaborate tricks.

Ann Radcliffe's *The Mysteries of Udolpho* (1794) was the first to utilize this motif. Its popularity resulted in numerous imitators (the most famous was *Northanger Abbey*, by Jane Austen, pubished in 1817), but it was Matthew Gregory Lewis that blew this formula out of the water. Drenched in supernatural events, satanism, and sadism (including the rape of a nun [!], among other things), *The Monk* (1796) became the most shocking novel of the century. The story consisted of two main plot threads that wove together. The main protagonist, Ambrosio, is portrayed as a respected clergyman in Madrid, who is visited and seduced by a demon in the form of a young and lovely woman. Under the influence of the demon, Ambrosio kills his mother and later rapes his sister on a bed of rotting corpses. In some ways, *The Monk* can be seen as the entire hardcore *ouvre* of Edward Lee and Wrath James White of 1796. It was certainly hardcore for its time, and as a result it was banned and suppressed in later editions.

These two polar opposites of the gothic archetype (*The Monk* and *The Mysteries of Udolpho*) were imitated by other writers hoping to cash in. From 1800 to roughly 1820, hundreds of these retreads were published in England, on cheap paper with lurid covers. These books became known as "shilling shockers" (so named because they cost one shilling). In a way, the shilling shocker can be seen as the first examples of pulp fiction. It has been argued that the extreme popularity of these novels led to the downfall of the gothic novel as an art form, but several seminal works were published during this later period: *Frankenstein* by Mary Wollstonecraft Shelly (1818), *Melmoth the Wanderer* by Charles Maturin (1820), and *The Confessions of a Justified Sinner* by James Hogg (1824). The last gasp of the form was probably *The Black Spider* by Jeremias Gotthelf (1842), *Jane Eyre* by Charlotte Bronte, and *Wuthering Heights* by Jane's sister, Emily.

Frankenstein, Jane Eyre, and *Wuthering Heights* have been written about and analyzed since their first publication and have remained in print throughout. The remaining three have been well-known to true aficionados of the genre. *Melmoth the Wanderer,* with its central narrative of a young man researching an ancestor who has been alive since the 16th century, who wanders the earth in search of someone willing to lay down their soul for him, is filled with gothic trappings: decaying castles and dungeons, ghosts, cannibalism, and deals with the devil. Hogg's *The Private Memoirs of a Justified Sinner* is the first novel in which the author went out of his way to give the story a ring of authenticity—a year prior to publication, he wrote a letter (anonymously) to *Blackwoods* magazine (then a popular London magazine that later published the works of many great writers of the supernatural) stating that a corpse had been found clutching an old manuscript in its fingers; the manuscript itself appears in the novel, with sufficient backstory to lend verisimilitude to the hoax. In a way, it was *The Blair Witch Project* of its time. The plot of the novel itself deals with the heir to the Laird of Dalcastle who is persecuted and later murdered by his half-brother, who succeeds him but later hangs himself; a hundred years later, his body is found along with his written confession.

Published in 1842, Jeremias Gotthelf's *The Black Spider* is about a pact with the devil that leads to a hideous creature that plagues and devastates a Swiss community one hundred years after it was initially bound by a curse. The imagery in the novel is vivid, and one scene during the climax is similar to a scene in the film *The Belivers* (1987) in which hundreds of spiders burst out of a boil on the heroine's cheek.

Gothic fiction was primarily written by Europeans, although it was read and enjoyed by Americans. What is most likely the first American-published horror novel is probably Charles Brockden Brown's *Wieland, or The Transformation* (1798). While *Wieland* has an obvious gothic influence, Brown set the narrative in his native America, a land without crumbling ruins and ancient castles, in a landscape that was relatively young in terms of its history (a significant motif of the gothic structure was the seed of the narrative was drenched in deep history, sometimes running back several hundred years). In the novel, the protagonists father, a missionary, invents his own religion and later dies mysteriously; a series of hauntings take place near the place where he'd built a bizarre temple for his religious cult. Like any good gothic novel, though, there is a rational, yet unexpected twist!

The gothic novels had a huge influence on the short story form as well, with the works of Nathaniel Hawthorne and Edgar Allan Poe being obvious examples. Poe originally mocked the gothic mode in his fiction; he later took the gothic archetype to great heights in "The Masque of the Red Death". Hawthorne's work is not often thought of as being in the gothic mode. Most academics classify his work as romanticism, or dark romanticism, which are cautionary tales that suggests guilt, sin, and evil are inherent in all human beings. However, Hawthorne's work in the horror mode certainly utilizes the gothic archetype in such tales as "Young Goodman Brown," Rappacini's Daughter," and "Ethan Brand," as does his novel *The House of the Seven Gables*.

Poe and Hawthorne's approach to the gothic was markedly different from each other and unique. Hawthorne tended to explore the Puritanism of his ancestors (Hawthorne's family was among the original colonists and much of his fiction is either set during this time, particularly during the Salem Witch Trials, or draws on their aftermath). Poe utilized the gothic motif primarily as atmosphere.

Poe and Hawthorne were wildly popular in the early Victorian-era, and their influence is still felt today. During their active periods, and in the years following their deaths, their work influenced a slew of writers on both sides of Atlantic—Joseph Sheridan Le Fanu, Fitz James O'Brien, and the collaborative team of Erckmann-Chatrian (French authors Emile Erckmann and Alexandre Chatrian). Poe was most certainly America's most famous and influential author of horror and the supernatural in the hundred years or so after his death. And while other writers dabbled in horror and ghost stories, none matched the gruesomeness or the pure horror Poe envisioned.

One writer who came very close to achieving Poe's mantle in the United States was Fitz James O'Brien. Born in Cork County, Ireland, in 1828, O'Brien emigrated to America around 1850 and began publishing poetry and short fiction in the leading magazines, newspapers, and journals of the day in the decade before the Civil War. Today he is most famous for a series of stories that were, in many ways, early forays into science-fiction, but were also clearly horror stories—"What Was It?—A Mystery," "The Child Who Loved a Grave," "The Diamond Lens," and "The Lost Room." One of the more interesting aspects of O'Brien was his idea to start a horror magazine in 1852! While the idea never gained traction (it was expressed anonymously in the December 1852 of The *American Whig*) it most certainly would have been an immediate failure, but it would have beaten *Weird Tales* to the punch by almost seventy years.

Despite producing fiction that was beginning to attract attention, O'Brien's life was cut short by the Civil War in 1862.

The 1860's were a quiet time for the development and publication of horror fiction and ghost stories. Most of the writers who dabbled in the genre hailed from across the pond— Irish writer Joseph Sheridan Le Fanu and the team of Erckman-Chatrain were the most significant during this period.

In the years following the Civil War, American writers were utilizing the changing landscape of the country—both figuratively and politically—in their fiction. While not thought of as a horror writer, the works of Herman Melville figure strong during this period, especially some of his shorter work (such as "Bartleby the Scrivener"). Known today as the author of *Moby Dick*, the novel that pretty much ended his career— *The Confidence Man: His Lives and Works* (1857) is really a stand-out piece of horror fiction that manages to unsettle and subvert. Nobody knew what to make of it in 1857, and it's only been within the last forty years that the novel has found a new audience who appreciate it for what it is—a great piece of American Literature.

As I've pointed out by citing the above mentioned works, the gothic mode did not die in 1820 as many scholars assert. Many academics believe the gothic mode was completely dead by the early Victorian era and had declined into the "Penny Dreadfuls" (sometimes referred to as "Penny Bloods"). Like the shilling shockers from forty years before, the Penny Dreadfuls were't really that dreadful by today's standards. But to Victorian sensibilities, some of them caused quite a sensation. One of the most infamous was James Rymer's gigantic serial novel *Varney the Vampire* (1846), which paved the way for countless vampire novels and stories including *Carmilla*, by J. Sheridan Le Fanu (1872), *Dracula* by Bram Stoker (1897), and pretty much every vampire story that was published in pulp magazines like *Weird Tales*.

(Of course, you all know that one of the earliest appearances of a vampire in horror literature was Dr. John William Polidori's short story, "The Vampyre," in 1819, written as part of that same challenge to write a terrifying ghost story that prompted then 17-year-old Mary Shelly to pen *Frankenstein*).

Because of the sensationalism so prevalent in the Penny Dreadfuls, the vast majority of them were dismissed by contemporary critics (and later academics) as cheap trash. Recently, however, several Penny Dreadfuls have undergone a sort of renaissance with modern readers and critics, and are now seen more favorably. Among them is the work of George W. M. Reynolds (a popular Penny Blood writer whose work often outsold the work of his contemporary, Charles Dickens), Thomas Prest, and James Malcom Rymer, author of *Varney the Vampire*, and who created the villain Sweeny Todd in his Penny Dreadful *A String of Pearls* (itself, often attributed to Thomas Prest).

A vast majority of the works cited above are in print, either through one of the major book publishers on both sides of the Atlantic, or through one of the many eBook publishers who are issuing public domain works (mostly for free, some for a small fee). Some of the short fiction mentioned herein can be found in any number of the reprint anthologies mentioned in the first installment of this column. Other sources include any number of Mary Danby's excellent anthologies from Octupus Books, which reprinted many early Victorian-era horror fiction.

Ghosts, *Conte Cruel,* and more Victorian era horror fiction

Part One of this column took us, quite literally, from the Stone Age to the mid-Victorian era in about 3,000 words. Not an easy task! In that previous installment I attempted to trace the beginning development of what we now recognize as horror fiction in literature by highlighting some classic works of Greek Epics ("The Illiad" and "The Odyssey"), to Shakespearean plays (*The Tragedy of Macbeth*) and on to the early Gothic novels (*The Monk, Melmoth the Wanderer*). Writers as diverse as Mary Shelly, James Hoog and Jeremias Gotthelf were touched on, all in an attempt to shine a light on some early examples of horror fiction.

When I left off at Part One I made brief mention of the Irish writer Fitz James O'Brien (who emigrated to the U.S. in 1852). Since O'Brien was killed in the U.S. Civil war, we can use that time period as an opening benchmark for this installment.

Shelly, Poe, Hawthorne, and O'Brien. Three of those names are well-known to the readers of this magazine. O'Brien is probably known to those few among you who are deeply read in the history of supernatural horror. Another writer who was producing quality work in the horror mode during this time period was another Irishman named Joseph Sheridan Le Fanu. Don't let that seemingly French surname fool you. Le Fanu's ancestry goes back to the Hugeunots, but he was Dublin born and raised. Le Fanu's early work began appearing in 1839. By 1864 he had produced a steady stream of novels and short stories, most of them in the mystery vein but quite a number of them clearly in the horror mode, particularly the ghost story. His novel *Uncle Silas* is a great mid-Victorian gothic melodrama involving an accusation of a sinister crime, a sinister governess, and family drama that would rival any modern day soap opera. Le Fanu's work is characterized by their slow, careful buildup that eventually evolve to terrifying conclusions. His most terrifying work, though, was at the novella length, particularly "Green Tea" (1869) and "Carmilla" (1871).

The years between 1872 and 1884 was a relatively quite one for horror fiction with most of the interesting work coming from the French, particuarly from the Decadent movement. The writing team of Emile Erckmann (1822–1899) and Alexandre Chatrian (1826–1890), active since the 1840's, produced steller work during this period ("The Murderer's Violin" and "The Queen of the Bees," both from their 1876 collection *The Man-Wolf and Other Tales*), as did Theophile Gautier ("The Mummy's Foot," from 1864). Villiers de l'Isle-Adam produced a short story collection that was the beginning of something that would be felt for the next hundred years—*Contes Cruels*.

Before we get further into the Decadent movement and the *conte cruel*, it should be noted that the dominant form of the gothic and the supernatural in literature throughout the Victorian era was the ghost story.

Writing in the *Penguin Encyclopedia of Horror and the Supernatural* (Viking Press, 1986), Jack Sullivan argues that the golden age of the ghost story was ushered in by the works of Edgar Allan Poe and J. Sheridan Le Fanu. Indeed, between the 1830s and around the start of World War I, the ghost story was the dominant form of the supernatural horror story. In addition to the work of Poe and Le Fanu, such writers as Mary Elizabeth Braddon, Harriet Prescott Spofford, Mrs. J. H. Riddell, Erckmann-Chatrian, Amelia B. Edwards, Wilkie Collins, Rudyard Kipling, and Edith Nesbit excelled at the form.

Many of the best practitioners of the ghost story were women, although this should come as no surprise. Women have been writing superior horror fiction since the time of the early gothics (Ann Radcliffe, the Bronte Sisters, Mary Shelly). During the mid to late Victorian era, women penned some of the most chilling and effective ghost stories, among them Charlotte Perkins-Gilman, Margaret Oliphant, and the aforementioned Ms. Braddon, Spofford, Edwards, and Nesbit. Using the Gothic archetype pioneered by Radcliffe and Poe, women could use this backdrop to explore darker themes in their fiction and weave themes of love, marriage, family, and motherhood along with death, madness, betrayal and sin. A good example of this is "Man-Size in Marble" by Edith Nesbit (1886). The story concerns a pair of newlyweds who move to a small village where they learn that the local church's marble statues come to life each year on All Saint's Eve to wreak revenge. The groom scoffs at this, of course. However, All Saint's Eve arrives, and he rushes to the church to find that the stone slabs that bear the statues are empty. What will happen to his wife?

"John Charrington's Wedding" (1891), also by Nesbit, revolves around the theme of marriage. John Charrington had been courting May and had repeatedly asked her to marry him only to be turned down. Then she says yes. Determined to marry her no matter what, John makes due on his promise in a way that will make your spine tingle.

Ghost stories weren't the only form of the supernatural story women excelled in. While Charlotte Perkins-Gilman penned her share of them, she is also known for writing one of the finest tales of psychological horror, "The Yellow Wallpaper". Perkins-Gilman was a prominent feminist and authored numerous essays and non-fiction books on feminism. Much of her fiction is colored with feminist leanings and "The Yellow Wallpaper" is no exception. Written in a first person epistolary style, the narrator is a woman whose physician husband has confined her to the upstairs bedroom of the home they have rented for the summer. She is forbidden to work, the windows of the room are barred, and there is a gate across the top of the stairs—essentially, her husband is controlling her access to the rest of the house. With nothing else to stimulate her intellectually, she becomes obsessed by the pattern and color of the wallpaper in the room she is confined in and begins to imagine there are women creeping around behind the patterns of it. Then she begins to think she is one of them.

"The Yellow Wallpaper" is one of the finest pieces of psychological horror. While there have been numerous feminist interpretations of it since its original publication (in 1893), and Perkins-Gilman explained that the story was influenced by her experience as a patient, it is also sometimes described as an example of gothic fiction due to its depiction of madness and powerlessness in its main character. In H. P. Lovecraft's landmark essay "Supernatural Horror in Literature," he writes "The Yellow Wallpaper rises to a classic level in subtly delineating the madness which crawls over a woman dwelling in the hideously papered room where a madwoman was once confined.".

During this period another mode of the horror tale was being developed by writers on both sides of the Atlantic. Previously, I'd mentioned the *conte cruel*. The literal translation for *contes cruels* is 'cruel tale. Stories in this mode usually contain some sort of horror of the physical sense (torture, violence, mental persecution, etc) and ends in a cruel twist of fate. An example of this is Villiers de l'Isle Adam's short story "The Torture by Hope" in which a condemned prisoner of the Spanish Inquisition (who has been tortured mercilessly in a dark basement) finds a moment to escape and makes a break for it. As he realizes he will be free from his torture, he becomes elated! However, the moment he sees freedom he also comes face to face with his Inquisitors who have only allowed him to escape so they could savor the moment of watching his sense of hope turn to horror as he realizes he's been captured.

Guy de Maupassant (1850–1893) was a French writer who produced stories of this nature. Much of de Maupassant's work was realistic in mode and the supernatural works he produced were often a metaphor for his protagonists' troubled minds. One example of this is "The Horla," which is about a man haunted by an invisible monster and burns his house down in an attempt to kill it. The narrator isn't sure if the monster lives or dies after the attempt, and because the creature is invisible there is no way to tell. Is there really a monster or is this all a product of the protagonist's mind?

Another French writer, Charles Baudelaire (1821–1867), is perhaps best known to lovers of dark fiction as the author of *Les Fleurs du mal* ("The Flowers of Evil"), a volume of poetry that was originally published in 1857. The themes of the poems range from death to decadence and eroticism. Baudelaire, along with with Theophile Gautier were greatly influenced by the romanticism of Edgar Allan Poe. The term "decadence" was originally used as a term by hostile critics towards some of these writers who labeled their works as such. Some of these writers later adopted the name, referring themselves as "decadents" as a badge of honor. Baudelaire and Gautier were among the first to link themselves with the term. Later writers of this period include J. K. Huysmans and Oscar Wilde.

The *conte cruel* was an outgrowth of the decadent movement, and this is clearly evident in Villiers de l'Isle Adam's collection *Contes Cruels*. The term *conte cruel* did not come into play until Villiers de l'Isle-Adam's collection was published. In the years that passed, the *conte cruel* as a term became to be known as stories with nasty twists, mostly nonsupernatural in nature. However, Villiers' collection was a mixture of both.

The *conte cruel* as a form was practiced by many writers associated with the decadent movement. While Poe may have unknowingly introduced it to America, the works of Ambrose Bierce (1842–1913?) and W. C. Morrow (1854–1923) are often thought to be the more likely writers who ushered this form of story in the United States. Tales like "The Middle

Toe of the Right Foot" and "An Occurrence at Owl Creek Bridge" by Bierce and "Over an Absinthe Bottle" and "A Game of Honor" by Morrow are some of their more well-known tales.

Bierce should be well known to horror aficionados. Born in 1842, he served in the Union Army during the Civil War. Stories like "An Occurrence at Owl Ridge" and "Chickamauga" were directly influenced by his war experience. In 1871 he moved to San Francisco, California and began a career as a journalist, writing for *The San Francisco Examiner*. It was there where he met W. C. Morrow. Both men were central figures in the San Francisco scene (which also included Frank Norris, Gertrude Atherton, Jack London, Bret Harte, and others). Bierce's short fiction is noted for its range—he wrote civil war stories, ghost stories, and tales that bordered on the psychological. There was a dry wit in many of his tales as well as a wicked sense of black humor. Bierce's books include dozens of short story collections, novels, and his collected works run eleven volumes!

W. C. Morrow is less well-known today. Born in Mobile, Alabama in 1854, Morrow made his way to California in 1879 where he met Bierce, who was just leaving his employment at *The Argonaut*, a literary journal based in San Francisco. At Bierce's encouragement, Morrow began selling his stories to *The Argonaut* and later sold his work to *The San Francisco Examiner*, where Bierce was also employed. While Morrow didn't produce as many works of fiction as Bierce, what little he did is of very high quality. Morrow and Bierce produced a handful of tales that can also be considered American *conte cruel* tales—specifically Morrow's "His Unconquerable Enemy" (in which a servant whose limbs have been amputated on the orders of a cruel rajah seeks revenge) and Bierce's "An Occurrence at Owl Creek Bridge".

Conte Cruel probably influenced the Grand Guignol theater in France which began to gain traction in the 1890's and continued on as late as the early 1960's. In its early years, French writer Maurice Level published numerous short stories in leading French magazines that were adapted to the Grand Guignol theater. Level is often seen as the heir of Villiers de l'Isle-Adam and with good reason. Level's work showed a level of tension that as often highlighted by depictions of physical horror. Much of his best work is psychological in nature. A good example of this is "In the Light of the Red Lamp". The main character of this story expresses his loss on the death of a lover with a visitor, which makes him feel better. After confessing to his friend that he's taken a picture of her on her death bed but hasn't been able to develop the film for fear of losing his mind, he convinces his friend to accompany him to the darkroom and begins developing the film, only to find something rather terrifying. This is as in-your-face as it could get in the early decades of the twentieth century and it's no wonder that many of Level's tales were adapted for the Grand Guignol, which was the forerunner of splatterfilms (Grand Guignol theater was incredibly gruesome, even when compared to today's tastes).

Later writers who employed the *conte cruel* in their works include George Fielding Eliot (whose 1928 *Weird Tales* story "The Copper Bowl" is an unflinching tale of torture by rats), Charles Birkin, Robert Bloch and, more recently, Joe R. Lansdale. The weird-menace pulp writers of the 1930's utilized the influence on the *conte cruel* and Grand Guignol to great effect in the pages of *Dime Mystery Magazine* and *Horror*

Stories. And while there is no evidence she wrote for the U.S. weird-menace pulps, British author R. R. Ryan (who was probably Denice Jeanette Bradley-Ryan based on research conducted by John Pelan), there are scenes of cruelty and violence in her three little known but excellent novels (*Freak Museum*, *Echo of a Curse*, and *The Subjugated Beast*) that are not only in the Grand Guignol style, but would rival anything being written by such modern master's of the extreme like Edward Lee today!

The Penny Dreadfuls (and their U.S. equilvalent the Dime Novels) of the mid to late 1800's published fiction that was considered lurid (but wasn't really that extreme) for their time. These publications were aimed at a lower-income and less educated readership. The term "raw heads and bloody bones" was a British pejorative during this period, and was used to differentiate the more genteel traditional ghost story from the more graphic horror tales that were beginning to emerge, especially those penned by writers such as Dick Donovan and Clive Pemberton. Indeed, Donovan's "The Cave of Blood" and "The Mystic Spell" are abound with full-fledged blood and gore, an excess that was very out of place for the late Victorian era. This approach was considered to be a conscious decision on the part of the writer to be lurid and vulgar. Most of the ghost story writers of this era did not write graphic horror of this type. Their approach was more subtle, an effort to "make your flesh creep". To resort to the "raw heads and bloody bones" type of graphic horror fiction that was gaining attention in the late Victorian period was, well, rather uncomely for those times.

While the ghost story and the *conte cruel* were being developed, horror fiction was also gaining maturity in the novel form. While the gothic mode still held sway, writers began to employ elements of adventure and early science fiction in their works (the term "science fiction" wasn't coined until 1926 by Hugo Gernsback). One such writer who managed to blend elements of both was Robert Louis Stevenson. Known primarily as the author of *Treasure Island*, his lone horror novel *The Strange Case of Doctor Jekyll and Mr. Hyde* remains a *tour-de-force* in the genre for its sheer brilliance. Written in three days, according to legend Stevenson burned an earlier, more gruesome, first draft on the urging of his wife, then rewrote it in a fever pitch over the course of the next six days. Published in 1886, the plot of *The Strange Case of Doctor Jekyll and Mr. Hyde* should be familiar with even those only fleetingly aware of the movie adaptations. It was a success upon publication and was immediately adapted to the stage. Several film adaptations followed, the earliest in 1908.

The short story and the novella were the most popular form of the horror story throughout the Victorian era, although many writers began branching out more into novels. British writer Oscar Wilde (1854–1900) wrote several notable and influential works during this period, most specifically *The Picture of Dorian Gray* (1890). The 1890's, in particular, was a banner year for horror fiction for the novel form and the short story. General fiction magazines like *Blackwoods* and *Scribner's* published all sorts of fiction including horror— ghost stories, tales of vampirism, werewolves and psychological horror. Early tales of cosmic horror began to appear from such writers as Arthur Machen and Robert W. Chambers (Lovecraft didn't invent cosmic horror contrary to popular belief). H. G. Wells, who began publishing during this period, penned numerous short works much of it horror-tinged; his novels *War of the Worlds* and *The Island of Doctor Moreau* are his two most important novels in the horror mode of the late nineteenth century. Robert W. Chambers, who later turned to romantic fiction to make a living, penned what is probably the most important collection of short fiction during this period, *The King in Yellow*. The first four stories "The Repairer of Reputations," "The Mask," "In the Court of the Dragon," and "The Yellow Sign" make mention of *The King in Yellow*, a fictitional play that drives those who read it insane. Its later influence on the works of H. P. Lovecraft was unmistakable.

Bram Stoker's *Dracula*, Arthur Machen's *The Hill of Dreams*, Richard Marsh's *The Beetle* (all 1897) and Henry James's *The Turn of the Screw* (1898) are the final major novel-length works of horror of the 19th century. James's novel is subtle and ambiguous, and while James made it clear it was a ghost story, it was also a tale of madness. It remains a classic example of the ghost story in the English language. *Dracula*, on the other hand, while also hewing closely to the gothic, was *not* subtle, and was very much a melodrama for its times. It's influence can be traced back to J. Sheridan Le Fanu's 1872 novella *Carmilla*, especially in its suggestion of lesbianism. *The Beetle* by Richard Marsh, about an ancient Egyptian Princess who transforms herself into a beetle in order to seek vengeance from a member of Parliament, was initially more successful commercially than Stoker's *Dracula*. It was even filmed before the 1922 Nosferatu (which was an unabashed ripoff of Stoker's *Dracula*) in 1919.

(As an aside, the only reason *Nosferatu* survives today is due to film pirates of the era who duped copies after Stoker's widow sought and won compensatory damages and destruction of all prints of the film during her legal action against F. W. Marnau, the director, who had not been granted the film rights to the Stoker novel—he went ahead and filmed it anyway under a different name!).

The horror genre was in for a number of changes as the century closed, although the writers of that time could not have foreseen it. Keep in mind that horror fiction was still not thought of as a 'genre'. Writers as diverse as Rudyard Kipling, Thomas Hardy, and Mark Twain dabbled in it. The story papers of the day (magazines that published nothing but short fiction) ran all types of fiction ranging in coming-of-age tales, romances, and adventure; most of the fiction published in these magazines at the time were aimed at a literate, educated readership. Fiction published in books (short story collections, anthologies, and novels) were geared toward this same readership. Horror fiction that emerged from English and American literature during this period (Poe, Dickens, Bierce, Wells, etc) was simply a thematic device. Even writers who excelled at this type of work such as Ambrose Bierce and J. Sheridan Le Fanu didn't think of themselves as "horror writers," much less "ghost story writers". And while the ghost story was gaining in popularity (brought on by the growing interest in spiritualism), ushering in newer voices like Barry Pain, John Buchan, Algernon Blackwood, and Bernard Capes, it was commonly published alongside more mainstream fare in the leading story magazines of the day.

Motion pictures were in their early development, with what is arguably the first horror film (*Le Manoir du Diable*) first appearing in 1896 from French director Georges Melies. Also in 1896, a New York City magazine publisher named

Frank Munsey revamped his fiction magazine *The Argosy*. Remarking to a friend and fellow publisher as they noted the vast array of fiction magazines crowding the newsstands that "the story is more important than the paper it is printed on," Munsey rebooted *The Argosy* (which had existed originally as a tabloid called *The Golden Argosy* that published adventure fiction for teenage boys) in a different size to match the slick-paper fiction magazines of the time yet with a paperstock consisting of untrimmed pulp paper. Munsey targeted an adult audience with the new issue, dated October 1896.

Thus, the pulp magazine was born.

Late Victorian and Edwardian Ghostly Fiction and Early Pulp Horror

T hose of you who are new to this mini-series should pick up back issues of *Lamplight* for Parts One and Two of this column. Both installments attempt to cover almost two thousand years of literary history in just under 7,000 words (okay, maybe only one hundred and fifty years if we count the birth of the horror novel as being Horace Walpole's 1864 novel *The Castle of Otranto*). We left off in Part Two with some words on some of the most influential works that helped shaped horror fiction—*Dracula*, *The Turn of the Screw*, *The King in Yellow*, *The War of the Worlds*, and *The Island of Dr. Moreau*. We also left off with a foreshadow on the birth of the pulp magazine.

While *The Argosy* was most definitely the first pulp magazine, it certainly wasn't the first *horror* pulp. That came much later. Within a few years of *The Argosy*'s debut, other enterprising publishers who wanted to emulate Frank Munsey's success launched their own pulp magazine titles. Some of the more successful ones were *The Popular Magazine* in 1903 and Munsey's own *All-Story* in 1905.

The fiction published in the early years of these pulp magazines was primarily adventure. Serialized fiction was the most popular form. Quite often, three or four novellas or full-length novels would be serialized in any given issue. More serious fiction continued to run in the slick-papered story magazines like *Pearson's* or *Scribner's*, but pulp magazines began attracting solid writers. Probably the first horror story published in a pulp magazine was Jack London's "A Thousand Deaths" in *The Black Cat* (May 1899). My standards of what constitutes a horror story is pretty broad, and this tale of a mad scientist who uses various scientific experiments to induce death and then resurrect himself back from the dead also has science fiction themes. It was also London's first story publication. Another early story that was clearly in the horror mode was "Manacled" by Stephen Crane, appearing in a 1900 issue of *The Argosy*. Upton Sinclair also published some short stories with horrific elements in *The Argosy* in the late 1890s.

Most short horror fiction was still being published in the slicks, especially in such magazines as *The Storyteller, Cosmopolitan, Scribner's*, and *Everybody's Magazine*, or in single-author collections. In the United Kingdom *The Strand* and *The Cornhill magazine* were the leading story magazines. *The Strand* is noted for publishing a goodly portion of Arthur Conan Doyle's Sherlock Holmes stories. Holmes and *The Strand* became so synonymous with each other that *The Strand* is still thought of today as a mystery magazine (it was never strictly a mystery magazine).

The ghost story remained the dominant form of the supernatural horror story as the nineteenth century turned into the twentieth. While the ghost story had always been popular, the form seemed to undergo a surge in popularity in the first few decades of the new century. Probably the most influential writer of the ghost story to emerge in this period was Montague Rhodes James (1862—1936), who published his fiction as M. R. James. James began reading ghost stories when he was in prep school (he became a provost at Eton College), with the works of J. Sheridan Le Fanu being his primary influence. He began publishing his own ghost stories in the 1890s, and in 1904 his first collection *Ghost Stories of an Antiquary* was published. Every story in this collection is a classic: "The Ash Tree"; "Oh Whistle and I'll Come to You, My Lad," "Lost Hearts," "Canon Albert's Scrapbook"; those are just a sampling of what you'll find in this slim volume. Still in print after one hundred years, the stories that comprise it are now often bundled with other larger collections of James's short fiction. In 2001 Ash-Tree Press issued *A Pleasing Terror*, a huge volume collecting *all* of James's short stories including story notes, fragments, non-fiction essays and a novel (thanks to the wonders of eBooks, Ash-Tree has reissued this volume in multiple eBook formats and I highly recommend getting a copy for your Kindle or Nook).

The influence of M. R. James on the ghost story has set the standard for what the ghost story is and what it should be. His main characters were usually clergymen, academics, or wealthy collectors who accidentally meddled in areas they never should have. Plots unwind as the main characters in a Jamesian story slowly uncover past secrets through researching old manuscripts, letters, or books. James built his stories slowly and methodically, often to very nasty or surprise endings. His influence was immeasurable—other writers in the James tradition during his lifetime include the Benson brothers (Edward, Robert, and Arthur), H. Russell Wakefield, L. P. Hartley, Mary Wilkins-Freeman, Edith Wharton, and John Metcalfe. Contemporary writers who have been influenced by M. R. James include Shirley Jackson, Robert Aickman, Ramsey Campbell, Susan Hill, Joyce Carol Oates and Peter Straub. Lesser-known writers who I feel have continued the James tradition into the twenty-first century include A. F. Kidd, Barbara Roden, and Reggie Oliver.

Next to M. R. James, Edward F. Benson (1867–1940) was one of the more widely known practitioners of the ghost story. Benson came from a dysfunctional family; this more than likely influenced the subject matter and themes of his and his brother's fictional efforts. The elder Benson was a well-known clergyman with a violent temper—it was reported that he ruled his family with an iron fist. The family was plagued with drama: their mother had a lesbian affair with their sister's best friend. The sister in question later tried to kill their mother. She later went insane and eventually died in an asylum. With family drama like that, no wonder the brothers channeled it out through writing horror and ghost stories.

The Benson brothers never married. And while they never had children they left behind a legacy of horror and ghostly fiction that has thrilled readers for decades.

Edward was the most prolific of the three brothers and published his works as E. F. Benson. His first collection *The Room in the Tower* (1912) contains one of his most famous stories, "Caterpillars," which are huge, ghostly caterpillars covered with cancerous sores and armed with rows of claws instead of feet. In the story, they haunt an Italian villa. The title story, "The Room in the Tower," is about a young man who visits a friend's house during the summer. He has had nightmares in which he visits this same house and experiences dread upon having to stay in a room in the home's tower. Everything in real life begins playing out as in his nightmare and he eventually encounters what is hidden in the room.

E. F. Benson published over a hundred stories in his lifetime from the 1900's until the mid 1930's, eventually collecting them in three additional volumes.

Edward's older brother, Arthur (A. C. Benson, 1862–1925), was a close friend of M. R. James and worked as a teacher at Eton. Most of his stories were allegories written to be read aloud to his students. Some of his most enduring stories are "The Uttermost Farthing," "The Slype House," and "Out of the Sea". The younger Benson brother, Robert (1871–1914), became a Catholic priest and eventually served under Pope Pius X. He wrote two volumes of ghost stories. His lone supernatural novel, *The Necromancers* (published in 1909) was about a man trying to communicate with his dead lover.

Ash-Tree Press has not only issued volumes of E. F. Benson's work, they've also issued a joint collection of Robert and Arthur Benson's work in a single volume: *Ghosts in the House.* Originally issued as limited edition hardcovers, all the Benson brothers work is now available as eBooks.

Much like the previous century, women wrote a very large chunk of superior ghost stories in the new century. Two U.S. born authors, Mary Wilkins-Freeman (1852–1930) and Edith Wharton (1862–1937), wrote numerous short stories and novels in the supernatural mode. Wilkins-Freeman began publishing short fiction in the 1890's and by 1903 her first collection of ghost stories *The Wind in the Rose Bush and Other Stories of the Supernatural* was published. Two of her most famous stories are "The Shadows on the Wall" and

"Luella Miller". The former is a creepy ghost story; the latter is one of the better tales of vampirism ever published; both stories have been anthologized numerous times. Edith Wharton was not only a Pulitzer Prize-winning American novelist and short story writer, she was also nominated for the Nobel Prize in Literature several times. Horror aficionados will know her by her excellent novella "Afterward" (1910), which is in the mode of Henry James's *The Turn of the Screw*. In it, a young couple buys a home in the English countryside to fix up. They want a home with character but they also want a house with a ghost. As the story progresses, they realizes the house doesn't have a ghost but there are ghostly occurrences. So is the house haunted? Or are *they* perhaps the ones who are haunted?

Writers who had gotten their start in the previous century were still producing quality work in the first decade or two of the 1900s—H. G. Wells, Ambrose Bierce, and Arthur Machen continued to publish stellar work (Machen would publish some of his finest stories in the 1900's). Writers as varied as Upton Sinclair, John Buchan, Barry Pain, R. Murray Gilchrist, M. P. Shiel, Violet Hunt, and Bernard Capes wrote excellent stories. One of the most-loved classics of horror and the supernatural was published in 1902—the short story "The Monkey's Paw" by W. W. Jacobs. W. F. Harvey's "August Heat" is not as well known, but just as memorable.

The Brits seemed to dominate the genre. Algernon Blackwood (1869–1951) wrote numerous classic stories of horror and the supernatural during this period. His novella "The Willows" (1907) is one of the finest supernatural horror stories in English Literature. Blackwood also penned a series of stories that are probably the first in the psychic-detective mode that would later be emulated by such pulp writers as Seabury Quinn, Manly Wade Wellman, and August Derleth. Modern day writers who have riffed on the theme of the supernatural sleuth include F. Paul Wilson—hey, I love Repairman Jack as much as the next guy, but Blackwood did it first.

In the United States, Ambrose Bierce was still contributing quality horror stories to various periodicals. Maryland native Edward Lucas White (1866–1934) wrote two of that decade's most memorable horror stories. "Lukundoo" (1907), is probably the most nightmarish ("Lukundoo" was reprinted in the second issue of *Lamplight*... go read it). Another of White's most memorable tales is "The House of the Nightmare". Originally published in 1906, this tale of a traveller who's car breaks down on a lonely country road and winds up spending the night in an old house at the invitation of a farmer and his harlipped son treads familiar paths for modern readers. But in 1906 the concept was new (and in 1906 cars were not a common a mode of transportation, either!). The story still manages to create a sensation of weird, supernatural atmosphere more than one hundred years later.

Book-length works published during the first ten years of the new century include the aforementioned *Ghost Stories of an Antiquary* by M. R. James (1904), *The Heart of Darkness* by Joseph Conrad (1902), *The House of Souls* by Arthur Machen (1906), *John Silence, Physician Extrardinary* by Algernon Blackwood (1908), *The Man Who Was Thursday* by G. K. Chesterton (1908), *The Purple Cloud* by M. P. Shiel (a post-apocolyptic horror novel originally published in 1901, probably one of the first), and two books by William Hope

Hodgson: *The House on the Borderland* (1908) and *The Boats of the "Glen Carrig"* (1907).

Hodgson (1877–1918) was a British author who produced a large body of work starting in 1904 when he began to publish short stories in various magazines. Many of his stories were sea stories based on his years as a sailor. While many of these were straight adventure tales, quite a number of them were horror stories: "The Voice in the Night," "Out of the Storm" and "The Mystery of the Derelict" are just a handful. His most enduring works are in the mode of Algernon Blackwood's John Silence stories focusing on Carnacki, a detective who investigated supernatural occurrences. The first Carnacki story to be published was "The Gateway of the Monster" in 1910. Six more followed between 1910 and 1912 and three more would not appear until the 1940's well after his untimely death in World War I.

His most famous work, however, is probably *The House on the Borderland*. Published in 1908, this novel about two friends who travel to Ireland on a fishing trip find a ruined house that contains the diary of a man who once owned it. The diary hints at an evil beyond another dimension. While not the first novel to contain elements of cosmic horror, *The House on the Borderland* proved to be a significant influence on H. P. Lovecraft. It was a radical departure from previous works that relied on the older gothic tropes and was a key influence on the development of the weird tale throughout the twentieth century.

Film was still a growing medium in the 1900s, with most of the horror films between 1901 and 1910 being produced by George Melies in France (Melies, if you remember from the last installment, produced/directed what is now recognized as the first horror film in 1896). The U.S. film industry during those early years of motion pictures was based in New York City. There was no Universal Studios, no Warner Brothers. In short, Hollywood wasn't even much of a town then; it was simply an outpost outside of Los Angeles. The Selig Polyscope Company out of Chicago produced the first film adaptation of *The Strange Case of Dr. Jekyll and Mr. Hyde* in 1908 as a 16 minute silent film. In 1909 the Biography Company brought out *The Sealed Room* from director D. W. Griffith (who would gain fame in 1915 with *Birth of a Nation*). Both films are now considered lost. Another early horror film that was considered lost for a number of years was Edison Studios' adaptation of *Frankenstein*. Released in 1910, *Frankenstein* was the first film adaptation of Shelly's novel and was thought lost for a number of years until a copy resurfaced in the 1970s when a private collector discovered he had owned a print since the 1950's.

But the printed word, specifically the short story, was where horror fiction still reigned. And while the ghost story was still the dominant mode of the supernatural tale, the *conte cruel* or "the raw heads and bloody bones" type of fiction was kept alive through the works of Maurice Level, Barry Pain, Ambrose Bierce, Dick Donovan and Clive Pemberton.

While novels and short story collections were still published primarily in hardcover (sans dust jackets for the most part), many novels were originally serialized in the leading story papers and the early pulp magazines of the day. Illustrated dust jackets began appearing on hardcover books in the years leading up to World War I. Prior to this, in the nineteenth century, artwork was used to illustrate short stories in magazines. Spot illustrations sometimes appeared as the fronts-piece in books. For horror fiction, the illustrations were sometimes as ghastly as the stories themselves. One of the earliest artists who illustrated numerous books was Aubrey Beardsley (1872–1898). His work was often labeled grotesque, morbid, sinister, and satanic—just the kind of artist I would want illustrating something of mine! Beardsley's style influenced those who came after him, including those who provided illustrations for the pulps in the 1930's and 1940's, specifically Hannes Bok and Virgil Finlay.

So while the ghost story continued to be the dominant form of the supernatural horror story, and American pulp magazines began publishing more horror fiction, the world was bracing for real-life horrors in the form of World War I. The United States wouldn't enter the war until 1917, but beginning in 1914 the output of horror and supernatural fiction dropped significantly (probably because the real-life horrors of the war put a damper on the public's appetite for it in fiction). Plus, there were casualties—Bram Stoker died in 1912 and Ambrose Bierce had been declared missing (but presumed dead) in 1913; Hodgson was a casualty of the war, and other writers either joined the war effort or supported it in other ways—as journalists (Arthur Machen wrote for the *Evening News* at the time). While never the most popular genre in the United States, the occasional horror story could still be found in pulp magazines during the war years—one writer who began contributing horror fiction to pulp magazines during this period was Tod Robbins (1888–1949). Robbins's most infamous story wouldn't be published until 1923, a tale of twisted cruelty called "Spurs" which would later serve as the basis of a movie that was released in 1932 that is still talked about today—*Freaks*.

By the time the war was over in November of 1918 the landscape was changing. Technology was rapidly accelerating. Thirty years before, most American homes didn't have electricity. By 1920 most private homes and business in small and large cities were being powered by it. Movies began to be played at larger venues, gradually shifting away from the nickelodians that dotted most cities to much larger and more elaborate theaters. Radio hadn't been invented yet—well, it was in the early stages of development. In the U.S., the Adamson Act in 1916 established the eight-hour work day making it the first federal law that regulated the hours of workers in private companies. The concept began to spread throughout the country (prior to that, despite the efforts of labor unions since the 1830's, ten to twelve hour working days were still the norm). Automobiles were now becoming the dominant mode of local transportation.

In the years following World War I these gradual changes led to people having more leisure time. It should come as no surprise that with this increase in leisure time, popular entertainment in the form of movies and the written word exploded—the number of books published certainly grew. The number of pulp magazine titles competing for space on the newsstand grew to the point that readers who were interested in sports could be entertained with stories from the pages of *Fight* magazine or *Baseball Stories*. Fans of mysteries had *Black Mask* or *Detective Fiction Weekly*; readers of romance had *Love Story*; and, of course, you could find just about anything in *All-Story* and *Argosy*.

While horror stories and science fiction and fantasy were often included in the pages of *Argosy* and *All-Story* as far back as 1899, there was not one regular outlet for this type of fiction until 1919. You may have thought *Weird Tales* was the first magazine to be devoted to fantasy and horror but you would be wrong—but only to a point. The *Thrill Book*, launched in March 1919 by Street & Smith, lasted until October of that year and published sixteen issues. Half the contents were devoted to supernatural horror and fantasy, the rest was mainstream fiction. The first issue contained "Wolf of the Steppes," a werewolf novella by Greye La Spina (who had been selling to other pulp magazines for a year or so prior; she would go on to become a prolific and very popular contributor to *Weird Tales*).

During its short run *The Thrill Book* published horror and fantasy fiction by the likes of Tod Robbins, Seabury Quinn, Murray Leinster, and H. Bedford Jones. One of the most well-known stories to appear in the magazine was *The Heads of Cerebus*, a science fiction novel by Francis Stevens.

The career of Francis Stevens is one that has intrigued me for years. Stevens was the pseudonym for Gertrude Barrows Bennett (1883—1848) and she is generally regarded as the first major female writer of fantasy and science fiction in the U.S. Sadly, she isn't well known today by contemporary readers. She published her first story in *The Argosy* in 1904. Following the deaths of her husband in 1910 and her father in 1918 in World War I, she began to care for her invalid mother, all the while raising her daughter. It was during this period when most of her works were published. Her output stopped in 1920. All total her novels, short stories, and novellas number just over a dozen but they proved to be highly influential. Case in point: "The Nightmare," published in *All-Story Weekly* in 1917 is set on an island where evolution has taken a different course. *The Land That Time Forgot* by

Edgar Rice Burroughs explores a similar theme, but it wasn't published until over a year later. Other notable works by Francis Stevens include the novels *Claimed*, *The Labyrinth*, and *The Citadel of Fear*.

The war was over. Europe was rebuilding and regrouping. America was entering a period that would be known as "the roaring 20's" where liquor was illegal, but bootlegging it made gangsters rich... and the loosening of regulations in the financial markets of the day led to even more riches being made. There was reason to celebrate and America took it! California was now the movie capital of the world and there were actual movie stars (Mary Pickford, Douglas Fairbanks). Ghost stories were still extremely popular with the reading public, perhaps even more so now in the years after the war and the increased interest in spiritualism that had risen. More pulp titles were appearing on the newsstands. And in 1923, four years after the birth and death of *The Thrill Book*, another pulp would help usher in a revival of the horror story, sweeping it out of its gothic past for good and dragging it into the twentieth century.

Weird Tales and its Influence, Weird-menace, Early Horror Movies and Radio Shows

First, an aside. I had intended to cover early horror films (particularly some notable silent films of the 1920's, the early 1930's popularity of such horror films as *Frankenstein* and *Dracula*, and radio shows, particularly an early regional horror radio program. Unfortunately, space considerations has forced me to abandon this. I do hope to touch on some of this in a future installment at some point.

In the first few years of the 1920s, horror and ghostly fiction continued to be published in the leading periodicals and short story collections of the day. Pulp magazines like *The Argosy* continued to publish them to increasing popularity. And in March 1923 the first issue of *Weird Tales* hit the magazine stands in the greater United States.

Weird Tales was the brainchild of Jacob Clark Henneberger. As a result of his experience as a college student in Lancaster, Pennsylvania, he caught the writing and publishing bug. After a stint in the Navy, by 1919 he was in Indianapolis working for a weekly newspaper. His college experience in Lancaster led to the formation of the magazine

College Humor, which sold at the whopping high price of 50 cents per copy. It became widely successful.

In 1922, Henneberger and J. M. Lansinger formed Rural Publications, Inc for the purpose of publishing two pulp magazines—*Real Detective Tales* and *Weird Tales.* Henneberger admitted that his only reason for starting *Weird Tales* was for nationally known writers such as Hamlin Garland and Ben Hecht to submit fiction to it (both writers had expressed interest in writing fantasy but held back due to fear of rejection from more conventional outlets). Alas, Garland and Hecht never submitted their work to *Weird Tales.* Henneberger hired Edwin Baird as the magazine's editor and with that first issue, dated March 1923, history was made.

You wouldn't know history was being made by looking at that first issue, though. Measuring 6" by 9" in size and at a 192 pages, it was priced high for a pulp magazine—25 cents (most pulp magazines in the 1920's were priced at 10 cents). The first issue contained 24 stories, its most notorious being the title story "Ooze" by Anthony M. Rud, about a monstrous wave of... well, ooze that swarmed out of a backwoods swamp and devoured everything in its path (this theme pre-dated similar stories like "Slime" by Joseph Payne Brennan, which was published in *Weird Tales* in 1953, the 1950's B-movie *The Blob,* and Stephen King's novella "The Raft"). There were no illustrations in that first issue. There was also the beginning of a serial by Otis Adelbert Kline (serials would run in every issue until 1940).

The second issue saw a change in the logo and the front cover design. A somewhat better story by Anthony M. Rud appeared in this issue—"A Square of Canvas". The winner of that issue, though, was "Beyond the Door" by J. Paul Suter.

Suter also contributed fiction to Henneberger's *Real Detective Tales*, and would go on to contribute to *Black Mask, Dime Detective, Detective Story,* and other mystery pulps. In "Beyond the Door," an emotionally stunted scientist is haunted by strange visions of a well in his basement. Upon gearing up the nerve to investigate, the story concludes in a way that brings to light a past crime he committed. Readers well-steeped in the genre will probably see what is coming well in advance of the ending, but the story is still very effective. I imagine in 1923 the effect would have been much greater.

The May 1923 issue saw another logo change, the size increase to a bedsheet size (8 1/2" by 11) and the page count shrink to 64. The cover illustrations during this period ranged from appallingly bad to dull and uninspiring. Baird was a mediocre editor; while he managed to select some very good fiction, much of what he published in the first 13 issues was just not very good. For every good story Baird published, there were ten bad ones; for every *really* good one (and there were a few), there were ten bad ones. You get the picture. Baird's only coup, as it turned out, was buying and publishing a number of stories by H. P. Lovecraft, beginning in the October 1923 issue.

By May of 1924, *Weird Tales* was in trouble. Despite yet another logo change and some improvements with the cover art, Baird's ineptitude as editor didn't help matters. He did not like Lovecraft's work and only bought and published them at the insistence of Henneberger. He also rejected Greye La Spina's "Invaders From the Dark" (which was bought by Baird's successor, Farnsworth Wright in 1924 and became one of the most popular stories to ever be published in the magazine). Baird had lost interest in editing the magazine. Newsstand sales weren't very good. Henneberger tried to drum up sales by commissioning a series of articles by Harry Houdini (one of them being a piece of fiction ghostwritten by Lovecraft), but even that failed.

Henneberger decided to reorganize the magazine. After publishing a large double issue (dated May-June-July 1924), he entered into an agreement with B. Cornelius, the owner of the printing company that printed the magazine. Baird was replaced by the magazine's first reader Farnsworth Wright. The magazine's offices moved to Chicago, where Wright lived. And in November 1924, the first issue edited by Wright appeared.

Prior to that November 1924 issue, *Weird Tales* had received some notoriety that gave it a boost in sales. A story by C. M. Eddy Jr. called "The Loved Dead" from the May-June-July issue raised the ire of several church groups and the Ku Klux Klan. The story is the first-person account of a man who works as an undertaker in order to be near the corpses; he's a necrophile. He recounts his life-long love for the dead, including a disturbing, repressive childhood, and by the story's end he has attracted the attention of his employer and the police. Ninety years after its publication, "The Loved Dead" still manages to strike a chord with modern readers.

Copies of that issue of *Weird Tales* were withdrawn from many points of sale. The magazine made headlines and surviving copies of the issue in question were immediately snapped up by those who would find it. That issue is now a rare collectors item (actually, every issue from 1923 to 1932 or so is a rare collector's item—especially the second issue—recent auctions of entire runs of *Weird Tales* have seen the price of the second issue alone sell at an average of $25,000!).

It can be safe to say that Farnsworth Wright ushered in the magazine's golden age that has been unmatched since the magazine's existence. The list of stories and contributors Wright published are too numerous to mention here. Needless to say, he published what we now recognize as classic works of horror and supernatural fiction from the likes of Lovecraft, Henry S. Whitehead, Greye La Spina, Robert E. Howard, Clark Ashton Smith, Donald Wandrei, August Derleth, Hugh B. Cave, Robert Bloch, Henry Kuttner, Mary Elizabeth Counselman, C. L. Moore, and too many to mention.

While *All Story* and *Argosy* continued to publish the occasional dark fantasy or horror story, the closest thing to a competitor *Weird Tales* faced in the 1920's was *Amazing Stories*, which launched in 1926. Recognized as the first science-fiction magazine, *Amazing Stories* was started by Hugo Gernsback (the coveted SF award The Hugo was named after him). In its first year, *Amazing Stories* published a lot of reprints by the likes of H. G. Wells, Edgar Allan Poe, and Edgar Rice Burroughs, but it quickly hit its stride by publishing original material. Because its focus was geared more toward science-fiction, it wasn't a direct competition to *Weird Tales*, which only occasionally published science-fiction. *Weird Tales* published a full gamut of weird fiction, everything from the traditional ghost story to adventure fantasy, as well as gothic horror, non supernatural horror, and stories that fit no category. A good example of this were the early stories of Robert E. Howard, specifically his Solomon Kane tales. Solomon Kane was a late 16th/early 17th century Puritan who wandered the world with no goal other than to vanquish evil in all forms. Howard would go on to create other iconic and influential fictional characters such as Kull of Atlantis, Bran Mak Morn, and his most famous—Conan the Barbarian.

The tales of Kull, Solomon Kane, Bran Mak Morn, and Conan saw the creation of a new genre—sword and sorcery.

While Howard's tales were gaining fans in the pages of *Weird Tales*, another writer was finding his short fiction always on the favorite lists of readers as well. Howard Phillips Lovecraft, who first appeared in *Weird Tales* in the October 1923 issue, saw his most influential story published in 1928—"The Call of Cthulhu".

Much has been written about Lovecraft, this particular story, and the entire sub-genre this story spawned—the Cthulhu Mythos—that to address this subject further would be redundant. I expect everybody reading this magazine to be familiar with Lovecraft and the Cthulhu Mythos. If not, then please head to your nearest bookstore or grab your mouse, choose the online bookstore of your choice, and buy *The Best of H. P. Lovecraft* or the anthology *Tales of the Cthulhu Mythos* right now and bring yourself up to speed.

Lovecraft's Cthulhu Mythos stories were an immediate hit in *Weird Tales*. While other tales of Lovecraft's received favorable feedback from readers ("The Outsider," "Pickman's Model"), "The Call of Cthulhu" was the start of something special. Prior to the story's publication, three other stories were published that hinted at things to come—"The Nameless City" (from a 1921 amateur publication), "The Festival" (1925), and "The Color Out of Space" (1927). The latter was published in *Amazing Stories*, and concerned a meteor that crashed on a rural New England farm many years ago that has been slowly draining the life force of everything in its vicinity.

Some of Lovecraft's friends and correspondents couldn't help but be influenced by the concepts introduced in these stories. The first of was penned by Frank Belknap Long ("The Space Eaters"), shortly after "The Call of Cthulhu" was published. Long followed this up with "The Hounds of Tindalos" (1929), in which a man has visions of mysterious canine creatures that dwell in the angles of time and are constantly seeking to break into our world through nightmares.

Soon other writers were jumping on the bandwagon, most notably August Dereleth, Clark Ashton Smith, and Robert E. Howard. Lovecraft followed up "The Call of Cthulhu" with "The Dunwich Horror" in 1929, further cementing his mythos.

Thus, the Cthulhu Mythos was born. That term wouldn't really be coined until much later, after Lovecraft's death, by August Derleth.

Throughout the 1920's, *Weird Tales* was the most significant pulp magazine that published horror and weird fiction. Traditional ghost stories still appeared in the slick paper magazines and in British publications like *Pearsons*, but *Weird Tales*'s influence was unmistakable. The occasional horror story continued to appear in other pulp magazines, but *Weird Tales* was the only pulp dedicated to the strange and bizarre. It took awhile, but imitators appeared not long after. The first was *Ghost Stories*, which debuted in 1926. It specialized in "true" ghost stories, most of them re-tellings of local folklore. It also reprinted classic ghost stories from the likes of Agatha Christie, A. M. Burrage, Algernon Blackwood and others.

Occasionally it published originals from the likes of E. F. Benson and the occasional *Weird Tales* writer (Victor Rousseau, Frank Belknap Long, etc). it lasted until 1931.

The most significant competitor to *Weird Tales* was *Strange Tales of Mystery and Imagination*. Published by the Clayton Magazine chain, its first issue appeared in 1931. Unfortunately, it would only last for seven issues (the last was dated January 1933). Many of *Weird Tales*'s top writers were lured to *Strange Tales* by the higher rate of pay for fiction (2 cents a word as opposed to WT's top rate of 1 cent a word). What differentiated the fiction from both magazines was the stories in *Strange Tales* were more action-oriented and relied less on atmosphere. Still, some noteworthy material appeared in its pages, including "The Return of the Sorcerer" by Clark Ashton Smith, "Cassius" by Henry S. Whitehead, "Wolves of Darkness" by Jack Williamson, and the short vampire novel "Murgunstrumm" by Hugh B. Cave.

It was during this period when there was a change of the overall mood and setting of horror fiction being published in the short form and in the novel form. No doubt, the influence of pulp fiction had a lot to do with this. Noteworthy novels and short story collections published in this period include *The Undying Monster* by Jesse Douglas Kerruish (1922), *The Smoking Leg and Other Stories* by John Metcalfe (1925), and *The Dark Chamber* by Leonard Cline (1927). Of course, novels published as straight mainstream fiction published during these years also qualified as influential and highly effective works of horror—*The Trial* by Franz Kafka (1925) immediately comes to mind. Probably one of the strangest novels published during the 1920's was *Medusa* by E. H. Visiak (1929). In this novel, a young man accompanies an expedition to the Indian Ocean to ransom captives from pirates. The pirate ship turns out to be empty except for a single madman who directs the would-be rescuers toward an ancient and evil monstrosity. Upon original publication, *Medusa* was a failure. It was reprinted almost forty years later in paperback. Karl Edward Wagner once described *Medusa* as "...the probable outcome of Herman Melville having written *Treasure Island* while tripping on LSD." Yes, it is that surreal, and that strange. And it works.

Horror was was popular with filmgoers (1931 was the year Universal Studios released two classics—*Frankenstein* and *Dracula*). It was beginning to make its mark on the radio airwaves, mostly with regional radio shows with programs like *Witch's Tale*. It was alive in the pages of *Weird Tales* and books. The occasional horror novel was still published by mainstream book publishers, but many were originally published in pulp magazines. Short story anthologies devoted to horror fiction began to appear in greater quantity at this time, the most notable being the *Not at Night* series from England, edited by Christine Campbell (covered in issue #1 of *Lamplight*) and the *Creeps* series (edited by Charles Birkin). The bulk of most horror short fiction, however, was now being published in pulp magazines as opposed to the more mainstream magazines and newspapers that had previously published ghost stories and other tales of terror.

While most pulp magazines were seen as trash (and to be honest, most of the fiction published in the pulps just wasn't very good and hasn't held up well), a group of pulp titles that emerged in 1933 were seen as pure pornographic filth. The first of these infamous titles, *Dime Mystery Magazine*, saw its debut in December 1932 under a slightly different title from Popular Publications, a pulp magazine publishing company started in 1930 by Harry Steeger, who saw the need to start a publishing company that would publish magazines that would allow for escapist fiction for readers mired in the woes of the Great Depression. *Dime Mystery Book* was modeled after one of Popular Publications other pulps, *Dime Detective*, which was general mystery pulp. The new title wasn't successful, however. Steeger revamped the magazine with the October 1933 issue, renaming the magazine *Dime Mystery Magazine*, and establishing a new editorial policy. Inspired by gothic melodrama and the Grand Guignol theatre, the fiction published in *Dime Mystery* was a combination of mystery and horror with heavy emphasize on physical horror—deformed villians, extreme torture and violence, with a dash of sex thrown in. Steeger managed to commission a novelette by popular pulp writer Hugh B. Cave for the first issue (Cave was already well-known to the readers of *Weird Tales* and *Strange Tales* for several high-quality stories and novellas). That first issue was a hit. Succeeding issues outsold it. By 1934 two sister titles had been added to capitalize on *Dime Mystery Magazine*'s success—*Terror Tales* and *Horror Stories*. Thus, the weird-menace sub-genre was formed.

I and others have written elsewhere that splatterpunk (or its bastard step-child "extreme horror") is not a recent trend. As witnessed from past columns, depictions of graphic violence and terror of the kind found in splatter/extreme fiction go all the way back to the late Victorian period. The material published in the leading weird-menace pulps pushed the envelope of decency for that time. These are the kind of magazines Edward Lee would be writing for if he was born fifty years earlier. With stories like "The Tongueless Horror,"

"Imp of Satan," and my personal favorite—"The Mole Men Want Your Eyes," the fiction that appeared in the weird-menace pulps were over-the-top gothic melodramas heavy on sex and sadism. They also had a formula—no matter how bizarre or supernatural the threat is to the main characters, it had to be explained rationally by the end of the story.

The success of *Dime Mystery Magazine*, *Terror Tales*, and *Horror Stories* brought imitators like *Strange Detective Magazine* and *Thrilling Mystery*, among others. The formulaic editorial restrictions imposed made for some pretty repetitious (and not very good) stories for the bulk of these magazines, and for years after their demise, stories originally published in the weird-menace pulps languished in obscurity. A handful of writers known mostly for their work in more "respectable" pulps (not that a magazine like *Weird Tales* was considered respectable to most people), most notably Hugh B. Cave, Arthur J. Burks, Robert E. Howard, and Henry Kuttner, wrote for the weird-menace pulps. Some rather talented folks wrote for the weird-menace pulps. One of them, John H. Knox, was a critically-acclaimed poet prior to turning his attention to the weird-menace pulps; another, Donald Dale (a pseudonym for Mary Dale Buckner, probably undertaken because it would freak out the largely male audience that a woman could get down and dirty like the guys) had a deep background in classic English Literature and wrote for the weird-menace pulps to support herself while working on her Ph.D. It is only recently due to the tireless efforts by anthologists—most notably Sheldon Jaffrey, Robert Weinberg, and John Pelan—that the good stuff that was published in the weird-menace pulps is being excavated and reprinted.

The settings for most horror films still relied heavily on the gothic. Only the short fiction published in the pulps, especially *Weird Tales*, appeared to be dragging the horror and supernatural story out of its gothic roots and into the twentieth century. Horror fiction published during that time began to have a more contemporary feel with those days—indeed, re-reading those stories now, one gets the sense many of them could be written today. The world was changing and horror fiction was changing with it. And as the world began to teeter toward the brink of another World War, a number of factors would help shape the horror genre into the form we all know and love today.

Horror in the Late 1930s and 1940s; British Thrillers, Weird Tales gets a New Editor, Arkham House, and Neglected Horror Writers of the War Years

The late 1930's was, by all accounts, a terrible time for the United States economy. If you were employed you were damn lucky to have work. And if you were among the almost 20% of the population who couldn't find work due to the Great Depression, things were dire. Of course, Roosevelt's New Deal and its various programs helped put people back to work, but it wasn't until World War II was in full swing that the economy seemed to bounce back. The war machine had to be fed, of course.

If you were a fan of horror fiction in 1939 you had a wealth of material at your fingers courtesy of your neighborhood newsstand every month. Had there been a *Year's Best Horror Stories* anthology series during that time its editor would have had to wade through 12 thick issues of *Weird Tales* as well as 6 issues each of *Horror Stories, Terror Tales, Dime Mystery Magazine*, and *Thrilling Mystery*. There was also *Argosy, Astounding, Amazing Stories* and other general fiction pulps, as well as titles like *Detective Fiction Weekly* and *Black Mask* that published the occasional macabre tale. 1939 saw the debut of two fantasy/horror pulps—*Unknown* and *Strange Stories* (we'll discuss these in a moment), putting further strain on our hypothetical Year's Best anthologist. And we haven't even taken the general slick magazines like *Collier's* or the occasional anthology or single-author collection into consideration.

In England, horror fiction continued to be popular with a segment of the population. The Brits still referred to it as ghostly fiction or supernatural fiction. The supernatural thriller reached its peak during the 1930s in Britain with the novels of Walter S. Masterman, Mark Hansom, Garnett Radcliff, and Edmund Snell being published and well-received on that end of the pond. Published in hardcover, these novels had elements of mystery, adventure, and supernatural terror (some of these novels were also reprinted in the United States) and primarily went into the British Library system to be enjoyed by readers who had no distinction on sub-genres of horror. Some of these writers, like Garnett Radcliff and Arlton Eadie, also wrote for such U. S. pulps as *Weird Tales* (Eadie's novel *The Trail of the Cloven Hoof* was serialized in *Weird Tales* over the span of 6 issues in 1936).

Here in the U.S., novels by Alexander Laing (*The Cadaver of Gideon Wyck*), William Sloane (*The Edge of Running Water*), A. Merritt (*Creep, Shadow!* and *Burn, Witch, Burn*) and Nathanael West (*Day of the Locust, Miss Lonleyhearts*) were all published by various NY Houses as general fiction (in the case of the two A. Merritt novels they were originally published in pulp magazines). They may have been published as regular mainstream fiction but they were clearly horror novels. Writers more known for mystery fiction such as Daphne Du Maurier and Agatha Christie also produced novels that I would consider horror in a heartbeat (*Rebecca* and *And Then There Were None*).

Lest you think the only quality horror fiction being produced was from the Brits and the Yanks, that wasn't the case. As demonstrated in previous installments when discussing the Gothic novel, German and French writers still played an active role in producing fine works of dark fiction, with the work of Hanns Heinz Ewers being most notable in the years prior to World War II. Ewers is known today for a number of excellent novels, among them *Der Zauberlehrling* (*The Sorcerer's Apprentice*, 1910; 1927 for the English translation) and *Alraune* (1911), an excellent and twisted reworking of the Frankenstein myth. Ewers also authored a number of effective short stories, his most notable being "The Spider" (1915). Polish writer Stefan Grabinski wrote a number of short stories and novellas in the 20s and 30s that saw English translations over the years, most specifically in the 1980s and 1990s. Two Japanese writers, Ryunosuke Akutagawa and Taro Hirai produced effective, weird, and, in some cases, disturbing works prior to World War II. Harai is better known under his pseudonym Edogawa Rampo, itself a play on the name of Edgar Allan Poe. His story "The Human Chair," originally published in Japanese in 1925 (with an English translation first being published in 1956), is probably his most well-known and most reprinted story. I didn't encounter it until the mid-1990s; I wish I'd encountered it earlier. And in the mid-1930's, Belgian writer Raymundus Joannes de Kremer (known to devotees of weird fiction as Jean Ray) penned a number of evocative, strange stories, some while he was serving a two year prison sentence for embezzlement (his most notable story "The Shadowy Street" was written while he was serving time). Some of his translated short fiction appeared in *Weird Tales* and a few of his stories were published under the pseudonym John Flanders in the weird-menace magazine *Terror Tales*. Like other non-native English speaking writers, Ray would not see a full English translation of his work in book form appear until decades later.

In 1939 the weird-menace pulps were still being published, but they had faced a backlash in 1937 over their extreme content and were now largely confined to under-the-counter sales. *Weird Tales* had changed hands; in mid 1938, J. C. Henneberger sold his share in the magazine to William J. Delany, a pulp magazine publisher based in New York. Delany published the very popular pulp magazine *Short Stories*. Henneberger sold his interest in *Weird Tales* on the condition that Delany retained Farnsworth Wright as editor and Delany accepted. However, Wright saw the writing on the wall and only remained with the magazine another two years. Shortly after he retired he succumbed to Parkinson's disease, which had afflicted him throughout his tenure as editor for *The Unique Magazine*.

His replacement was the magazine's assistant editor. Dorothy McIlwraith was a very compenent editor of *Short Stories* magazine when she was tapped to assist Wright during *Weird Tales*'s transition. With Wright's resignation, she stepped into his position effortlessly. Her tenure with the magazine is overshadowed by Wright's in many ways, but she was a great editor who carried the magazine into the 1940's until its demise with the September 1954 issue. It was Dorothy MacIllrath who nurtured and discovered the works of Theodore Sturgeon, Ray Bradbury, Joseph Payne Brennan, and Fritz Leiber, infusing new blood into the magazine. From the old guard she continued to publish the work of Robert Bloch, Manly Wade Wellman, Henry Kuttner, August Derleth, and Mary Elizabeth Counselman. She was also able to coax some of the *very* old guard back into the magazine—Greye La Spina and Everil Worrell published a number of tales during her tenure (she also managed to publish the occasional Clark Ashton Smith story, as long as it was non sword and sorcery... rumor has it the magazine's new owner didn't care for it and MacIllrath was not allowed to publish it). She published the work of authors that never appeared in any other magazine during this time, writers who proved to be very popular with the WT readership (Harold Lawlor and Allison V. Harding being two who produced some very good work). She is often under-appreciated by loyalists of the Farnsworth Wright era. It was her eye for talent and her own determination to find the best talent she could, even during the magazine's downward spiral in the early 1950's, that kept the magazine going until it finally ceased publication in 1954.

In early 1939 two new pulps devoted to fantasy and horror debuted. *Strange Stories* was launched as a direct competition to *Weird Tales*. It lasted two years. Content wise, *Strange Stories* often published stories that were rejected by *Weird Tales*. Despite this somewhat negative connotation, some true gems appeared in its pages including "For Fear of Little Men" by Manly Wade Wellman and "Logoda's Heads" by August Derleth.

More influential in the long-term was *Unknown* (in 1941 it underwent a name change to *Unknown Worlds*). Started by former *Astounding* editor John W. Campbell, *Unknown* was launched to provide a venue for groundbreaking tales of fantasy and horror. Campbell wanted his writers to focus on the contemporary; he wanted fresh voices. Therefore, it should come as no surprise that he would attract the talent of newer writers like Bloch, Sturgeon and Leiber, as well as *Weird Tales* mainstays like Manly Wade Wellman. Also featured very prominently in *Unknown* was the work of L. Ron Hubbard. Primarily known now as the founder of Scientology, Hubbard was a capable journeyman pulp author who wrote for the general fiction markets like *Argosy* and *All Story*; he also wrote westerns, romance, science fiction, aviation stories, mysteries, and adventure fiction. For *Unknown*, Hubbard contributed stories and short novels that are now considered horror and science fiction classics: *Fear*, and *Typewriter in the Sky*.

As an aside, Campbell was also a writer in his own right; a number of his tales appeared throughout the 1930s under his own name and various pseudonyms. His most famous tale is "Who Goes There?" which became the basis for two very classic films: *The Thing From Another World* (1951) and *The Thing* (1982; John Carpenter). The 1982 film version sticks closer to the original novella than the 1951 version does, but each version is excellent.

Another writer who deserves mention here is Jane Rice. Relatively unknown today, Rice is primarily known for the super creepy story "The Idol of the Flies," which appeared in the pages of *Unknown Worlds* in 1942. All total, she had a number of stories appear in its pages, as well as in *Charm* and *The Magazine of Fantasy & Science Fiction* in the 1950s.

As the United States formally entered the war in 1941, several things happened that helped spurn the death of the pulp magazines. The first was the paper shortages. The war effort saw the government step in and impose rationing on everything from food to tires to paper. Due to the paper shortages, publishers were forced to cut titles. Many magazines switched from monthly to bi-monthly or went to digest size. Some went out of business altogether.

The war also affected the British publishing industry very hard. The British thriller that had been so popular in the 1930s suddenly ceased as England entered the war. One of the best horror novels published during this time period suffered for being in the wrong place at the wrong time. *Dark Sanctuary* by H. B. Gregory was published in 1940 in a small hardcover edition of 400 copies, the standard issue at the time, which would have the majority of the books go out into the library system. *Dark Sanctuary* is a dark, brooding, gothic tale of a family curse and it hints at Lovecraftian cosmic horror. Unfortunately, shortly after its publication, the warehouse where the books were stored in preparation for distribution was destroyed during the Blitz. It is estimated that a few dozen copies survived by the simple matter of making it out of the warehouse (some to early buyers, others to the author himself). Over forty years later, one copy eventually wound up in the hands of Karl Edward Wagner, and when it showed up on his list of 'The 13 Best Supernatural Horror Novels' in a 1983 *Twilight Zone* column, it drove bibliophiles and aficionados nuts. This was before the Internet, so there was no way of jumping on to Abebooks.com or Amazon to learn more about it. Many people thought this book (and several others on Karl's list) were fake. Virtually unobtainable for over 60 years, *Dark Sanctuary* was finally reprinted in 2002 by Midnight House and is now available as a print on demand trade paperback from Dancing Tuatara Press.

With *Unknown* and *Weird Tales* still available on the news-stands, horror fiction gained an ally in the book publishing world. Formed in 1939 to preserve the works of H. P. Lovecraft (who had died in 1937), August Derleth and Donald Wandrei formed Arkham House and issued *The Outsider and Others*, the best of Lovecraft's fiction (Derleth and Wandrei were among the so-called Lovecraft circle of writers who all corresponded with each other and with Lovecraft by mail). Priced at $5.00 in an edition of just under 1,300 copies, it took five years to sell out. Undaunted, Derleth published a collection of his own stories under the imprint and then issued a collection by Clark Ashton Smith—*Out of Space and Time* (1942). Little by little, Arkham House began to gain an audience. Relying on a small stable of writers from the *Weird Tales* circle, Derleth cultivated those relationships and solicited short story collections out of them. His efforts resulted in such now classic works as *Jumbee and Other Uncanny Tales* and *West India Lights* (Henry S. Whitehead, 1944 and 1946 respectively), *The Opener of the Way* (Robert Bloch, 1945), *The Hounds of Tindalos* (Frank Belknap Long, 1946), and *Night's Black Agents* (Fritz Leiber, 1947). He solicited material from the best from Britian's writers—*Fearful Pleasures* (A. E. Coppard, 1946), *This Mortal Coil* (Cynthia Asquith, 1947), *The Clock Strikes Twelve* (H. Russell Wakefield, 1946). In 1945, Arkham House published their first novel, the now classic *Witch House* by Evangeline Walton.

Once that first Lovecraft collection was sold out, Arkham House issued another one in 1943 (*Beyond the Wall of Sleep*); in 1946 Arkham House did with Robert E. Howard what they did with preserving Lovecraft by bringing out *Skull-face and Others*, the first volume to collect Robert E. Howard's fiction. By this time, Arkham House was being run largely by Derleth (Wandrei stepped away from the firm when he entered the military in World War II and formally resigned after the war). In 1947 Derleth published the first book by a man who would go on to be a treasure in the fantasy community and in American Literature.

When one thinks of Ray Bradbury today they generally associate him as the author of numerous classic works of science fiction—*Fahrenheit 451*, *The Illustrated Man*, *The Golden Apples of the Sun*. These and many more volumes are beloved classics of fantasy and science fiction and Bradbury was a master at the form. But Bradbury was first and foremost a horror writer as evidenced by his very first book, *Dark Carnival*, published by Arkham House in 1947. At the time of its publication Bradbury was already branching out into the mainstream, with stories appearing in such slick publications as *Cosmopolitan* and *Harper's*. *Dark Carnival* contains some of these dark stories that appeared in these prestigious magazines, but the majority of the reprints comprise of the creepy stories he wrote for *Weird Tales* and *Dime Mystery Magazine* throughout the early to mid 1940's, stories that should be read by every serious student of horror: "The Small Assassin," "The Jar," "The Scythe," "The Smiling People," and "The Crowd".

Stories like "The Smiling People" were later considered by Bradbury to be too gruesome for further preservation, and he cut a number of these more "gruesome" stories out of the contents of *The October Country* (1955), his first mass market horror collection, which essentially reprinted more than half of the contents of *Dark Carnival* and included some recent efforts. Bradbury even toned down the more gruesome elements in such stories as "The Jar" and "The Scythe" for their appearance in *The October Country*. Want to read the original versions? Today you'll have to plunk down some serious cash. While Bradbury did authorize a reprinting of *Dark Carnival* in 2001 (from Gauntlet Press), that volume is now out of print. Still, it commands less prohibitive prices as the Arkham House edition on the secondary market. The eight or so remaining tales that were not reprinted in *The October Country* were eventually reprinted in several later collections (most notably *The Stories of Ray Bradbury* and *Bradbury Stories: 100 of His Most Celebrated Tales*).

Some notable horror novels published during the war years and in the mid to late 1940s include *Conjure Wife* by Fritz Leiber, *Night Has a Thousand Eyes* and *Black Alibi* by Cornell Woolrich, *The Screaming Mimi* by Fredric Brown, *Deliver Me From Eva* by Paul Bailey, and *Darker Than You Think* by Jack Williamson (that was by no means an exhaustive list... there were plenty of very good horror novels and single author collections published during this period). The short fiction of Robert Bloch and Fritz Leiber must be brought to light as well. Bloch started his long career while under the influence of his mentor H. P. Lovecraft in 1934. After publishing a number of notable Lovecraftian pastiches in *Weird Tales*, he quickly developed his own unique voice in the late 1930s and by the war years was producing notable, effective tales of horror, science fiction and fantasy. Some of his more stronger horror tales were collected in the previously mentioned *The Opener of the Way*, which was later included in the retrospective volume *The Early Fears* (1994). Fritz Leiber also bears mentioning. Leiber's prose was more lyrical and stronger than Bloch's (Bloch often reminded me of a 1940's Stephen King in many ways; his prose wasn't fancy, he simply wrote in a very direct manner that appealed to the common man), and he wasn't as prolific as Bloch, but the few works in the horror mode during the war years cannot be underestimated. His "Smoke Ghost" (*Unknown Worlds*, 1941) dragged the classic ghost story kicking and screaming out of the traditional Jamesian mode into the modern. It was a tremendous influence on the field that is still being felt today. Other influential work by Leiber in the horror mode in the early 1940s included "The Hill and the Hole," "The Hound" (1942), "Mr. Bauer and the Atoms" (1946) and "Diary in the Snow" (1947) among others.

One author that was probably not on the radar of most U.S. fans was R. R. Ryan.

Ryan is known today for authoring three exceptional horror novels—*Echo of a Curse*, *The Subjugated Beast*, and *Freak Museum*. In total, she published over eleven novels. And yes, I used the feminine pronoun 'she'. For years the identity of R. R. Ryan was unknown. An excellent essay by Ramsey Campbell on the novels of Ryan included a surmise that Ryan was female. D. H. Olson comes to this conclusion as well in his introduction to the 2002 reprint of *Echo of a Curse* when he surmises that Ryan was female "due to Ryan's inability to depict convincing male characters, while her female characters are much more fully drawn," as well as "significant examples of typically female outlooks and attitudes pervading even the most male dominating of her novels." Karl Edward Wagner, who first called attention to Ryan's work by including the three novels I've just named on his infamous "13 Best" list, also believed Ryan was female for the same reason as Olson (Ryan was the only author who appeared on all three lists; The 13 Best Supernatural Horror novels, the 13 Best Science Fictional Horror Novels, and the 13 Best Non-Supernatural Horror Novels).

And while there's still no documented proof, recent research into the matter tells us that Wagner, Campbell, Olson and John Pelan (who provides introductions to reprints of *The Subjugated Beast* and *Freak Museum*) might very well be right: it is believed R. R. Ryan was one of several pseudonyms used by Denice Jeanette Bradley-Ryan (proof that she was Ryan comes from her son). Why the pseudonym? Better yet, why does existing paperwork indicate that her father, Evelyn Bradley (then a rather well-known stage actor who later committed suicide in 1950) was the author? We'll probably never really know. Pelan surmises that Bradley-Ryan wrote the novels and her father handled the business end of publication for his daughter, hence the reason why the paperwork was in his name. The argument is surely convincing. And *Echo of a Curse* does read as if it were written by a woman. While there is a long history of female authors of ghost stories writing under their initials (or even taking on their husbands' names), and female authors who wrote fantasy and science fiction often used their initials (C. L. Moore comes to mind), in the case of Bradley the subject matter might have been the likely reason for the R. R. Ryan pen name. The level of cruelty depicted in *Echo of a Curse* is so strong that it will shock even today's most jaded Edward Lee fan.

The 1940s saw several ground-breaking anthologies published. Most notable was *Great Tales of Terror and the Supernatural* edited by Herbert A. Wise and Phyllis Fraser (discussed in an earlier installment). Another massive all-inclusive anthology was edited by none other than screen legend Boris Karloff. His mammoth anthology *And the Darkness Falls* contained not only the great ghost stories and horror classics, but also dark fiction and poetry by the likes of W. Somerset Maugham, Robert Browning, W. B. Yeats, Stephen Crane, and Joseph Conrad.

The anthologies of August Derleth must be mentioned in this space. Hopefully those of you reading this know that August Derleth was an accomplished writer in his own right—award winning regional novelist, accomplished writer of mysteries, and a very dependable and popular writer of horror fiction for *Weird Tales* and other pulps, Derleth had been writing professionally for over thirteen years when he co-founded Arkham House. Much has been made of Derleth co-opting Lovecraft's creations into something Lovecraft never intended (the short version: as an atheist, Lovecraft saw his Elder Gods as uncaring powerful interdimensional beings; as a Catholic, Derleth's own mythos fiction attempted to mold Lovecraft's fictional deities into a standard Christian archetype of good over evil). With a few exceptions, most of his mythos fiction is substandard, but he was a hell of an anthologist (and he excelled at the ghost story). His three hardcover anthologies for New York imprint Rinehart (*Sleep No More: Twenty Masterpieces for the Connoisseur, Who Knocks? Twenty Masterpieces of the Spectral for the Connoisseur,* and *The Night Side: Masterpieces of the Strange & Terrible*) are essential volumes in that they not only feature the usual classics, Derleth also includes what were then more contemporary tales by his comrades in *Weird Tales*: Carl Jacobi, Robert Bloch, Jack Snow, Ray Bradbury, Mary Elizabeth Counselman, and other talented writers from the *Weird Tales* era. Derleth would go on to edit over a dozen more anthologies, many of them under his Arkham House imprint, until his death in 1971.

I'm nearing the end of my word allotment for this installment. Needless to say, there was more to be excited about in regards to dark fiction in the 1940s too—there was movies, the emergence of such writers as John Collier, Shirley Jackson, and Flannery O'Conner in the slick magazines, and a new medium—comic books! We'll explore all that and how the Cold War and the threat of nuclear annihilation influenced and changed horror fiction forever.

The Death of *Weird Tales*, the Rise of Digest-size Science-fiction Pulps, Comics, *Playboy* and other Slick Paper Magazines, Richard Matheson, and Charles Beaumont

W*eird Tales* continued on throughout the rest of the 1940s, but it was now reduced to a bi-monthly schedule. Other pulps occasionally published horror during this time, most notably *Fantastic Adventures* and *Dime Mystery Magazine*. A pulp called *Famous Fantastic Mysteries* first appeared in 1939 and continued until 1953; it specialized in reprinting classic and neglected works from the past, particularly material that had appeared in the early years of the 20th century. It introduced new readers to the works of E. F. Benson and William Hope Hodgson, but it occasionally published new material ("The Man Who Collected Poe" by Robert Bloch is a notable example).

Despite the presence of so much good horror fiction in the pulps, dark fiction was represented in the slick paper magazines in the 1940s as well. "The Slicks" was a term many pulp writers used to refer to the general interest magazines printed on slick or glossy paper—*Collier's, The Saturday*

Evening Post, Liberty, American Mercury. They actually predate the pulps, having been around since 1850 or so. Slick magazines paid better rates to writers than the pulps. There was also a sense of pedigree when one had a story published in one of the slicks—Ernest Hemingway and John Steinbeck wrote for the slicks. You get the picture.

Slick magazines have always published science-fiction, fantasy, mystery, and horror fiction, but the pulps quickly became more known for genre fiction. However, throughout this time the slicks still published the occasional genre piece. Magazines like *The Saturday Evening Post, Charm* and *Collier's* published dark fantasy and horror with regularity throughout the 1940's and into the 1950s. British fantasist John Collier was a slick magazine regular. His "Thus I Refute Beelzy" is one of the classic 'deal-with-the-devil' stories that is much imitated. One writer who is sadly neglected today who appeared in the slicks is Gerald Kersh. Born in England in 1911, Kersh began publishing short stories in British publications in the 1930s. He authored over one hundred stories and dozens of novels of suspense and horror. One of his most well-known novels is *Night and the City* (filmed in 1957). He should be well-known to horror aficionados for the creepy and under-appreciated novelette "Men Without Bones," which appeared in a 1954 issue of *Esquire*.

Another notable writer who published short fiction in the slicks was Shirley Jackson. Jackson began publishing short fiction in the late 1930s, selling her work to literary journals and later graduating to such markets as *Charm, The Saturday Evening Post*, and *The New Yorker*. Her work was heavily imbued with symbolism and was steeped in the gothic tradition. Her most famous story, "The Lottery," appeared in the

July 1948 issue of *The New Yorker* and so outraged and disturbed readers that reaction to it made national headlines. Another tale that comes very close to the gut punch evoked by "The Lottery" is Roald Dahl's "Man From the South," which appeared in *Collier's* that same year. "Man From the South" is the story of a man who likes to place wagers. For the person who loses, well, they lose more than a monetary thing. They usually lose something more personal. It was famously adapted as an episode of *Alfred Hitchcock Presents* in 1960.

Also productive during this time period was Flannery O'Conner. Like Shirley Jackson, O'Conner's work is imbued with a sense of the gothic (she has been credited as being one of the founders of Southern Gothic). Much of her work presents a dark worldview despite her Christian background. While she did not like being referred to as a "horror writer" (if anything, she was clearly a mainstream writer, much like Shirley Jackson and, later, Joyce Carol Oates), she wasn't afraid to address horrific, bleak themes. One of her most famous stories is "A Good Man is Hard to Find," in which a grandmother, traveling with family to Florida, convinces them to visit relatives in Florida instead. The story slips into the horrific when they encounter escaped killers on the backroads.

After a period of absence, horror movies began to gain favor with film audiences during the tail end of the depression. Today's film audiences complain of the endless sequels and remakes Hollywood foists on us and it was no different back then. *Dracula* and *The Mummy* underwent numerous sequels throughout the 1940s. In 1941 Universal released *The Wolfman*, which helped cement much of the werewolf mythos we know today in modern werewolf fiction. A few years later Universal saw the need to put the Wolfman against Frankenstein and Dracula in *Abbot and Costello Meet Frankenstein* (despite the title, all of the Universal monsters made appearances, even the Wolfman and the Mummy). This trend continued during the war years until audiences grew tired of it.

Despite this, there were some genuinely good, effective horror movies that were released during this time. *Cat People* (1942), *The Uninvited* (1943) and *Dead of Night* (1945) were among some of the more memorable ones. Probably some of the best and most affective films that I certainly consider as horror were the works of Alfred Hitchcock, specifically *Shadow of a Doubt, Laura,* and *Notorious.* Hitchcock's debut as a director was an adaptation of Marie Belloc Lowndes novel *The Lodger* in 1927 (a minor classic of horror in its own right). By the 1940s Hitchcock was in demand in the Hollywood film industry as a director of mystery and suspense films, so by the time World War II was underway he was already seen as a first-rate Hollywood film director.

As the new decade dawned, so the culture begin to change. With the end of the war and the emergence of a new superpower in the form of the Soviet Union, one that was ideologically opposed to the United States and that possessed nuclear weapons, it brought a change of atmosphere to the collective United States population. This was reflected in much of the art, films, and novels and short stories published in this period. And as the 1940s gave way to the 1950s, this growing paranoia over communism would be reflected in film, the printed word, and in comic books and would inspire a fusing of two genres of the fantastic—science-fiction and horror.

Of course, science fiction and horror have intermingled with each other since the works of E. T. A. Hoffman and Mary Shelley, with the link becoming more intertwined during the pulp era. Yet a strange thing happened during the pulp era too... tales of science fiction became so distinct thanks to pulps like *Amazing Stories* and *Astounding Science Fiction*, the genre of science fiction became one of the more popular genres with the reading public (general fiction pulps like *All-Story* and *The Argosy* had been publishing science-fiction and fantasy since the 1900s). It became so popular that fans of this type of material began corresponding with each other, finding each other in the classified sections of the leading pulp magazines of the day. Eventually, a few enterprising fans got together and put together the World Science Fiction Convention in 1939. Held in New York, 200 people attended this inaugural event (in 1937, a science fiction convention was held in Great Britain with Arthur C. Clarke and Eric Frank Russell as guests of honor, so I guess that would count as the first official science fiction convention). Two more World Science Fiction Conventions were held in Chicago (1940) and Denver (1941) until World War II intervened. The convention resumed in 1946 and has been held every year since then.

Because fans of science fiction and fantasy (and horror) often read the same publications and many writers were not confined to one genre, you could say that the first World Science Fiction Convention in 1939 was the birthplace of the "Con". As the decades passed, regional SF conventions were formed and continue to this day. Science fiction was the dominant genre interest for most of the fans who attended these conventions, but it wasn't unusual to see writers known for their horror fiction attending them either. It wouldn't be until 1975 when a convention celebrating the darker side of fantasy was introduced... but we'll get to that in due time.

Science fiction was the perfect genre for writers who wanted to explore the themes confronting society during the Cold War years. Ray Bradbury, by then the premiere author of science fiction and dark fantasy, became the quintessential name associated with the genre. Other writers who wrote and published horror also wrote science fiction—Jack Finney, Robert Bloch, Eric Frank Russell, Henry Kuttner and his wife Catherine Moore (C. L. Moore). And as the calendar turned from 1949 to 1950 and a new decade began, the science-fiction/horror hybrid strengthened.

The year 1949 saw the debut issue of a new digest-sized pulp magazine called *The Magazine of Fantasy*, edited by Anthony Boucher and J. Francis McComas. By the second issue, the magazine was renamed *The Magazine of Fantasy and Science Fiction*. The first few issues of the magazine featured stories by the usual talent who contributed to the other pulp magazines of the day, but by the time the Summer 1950 issue rolled around a new by-line would appear, one that would grow steadily more popular and prove to become a huge influence on science fiction and horror.

"Born of Man and Woman" was the first professionally published story by Richard Matheson. This very short story is written in the form of a diary in very broken English. It is the account of an apparently deformed child who is kept chained in the basement by its parents and frequently beaten. Occasionally the child is able to pull its chain out of the wall and observe what's going on outside through the basement window. To reveal more about the story would spoil it for those of you who haven't read it (and you really should read it). Suffice to say, "Born of Man and Woman" was ground-breaking in many ways. It was compact and concise and its depiction of a monstrous child elicited both horror and sympathy. Within a few years, Matheson had established himself as a very capable and dependable writer of science-fiction, fantasy, horror, crime/mystery, and westerns, appearing in numerous pulp magazines in the early to mid 1950s. Like Ray Bradbury and Robert Bloch before him, his characters were normal people, archetypical middle-class Americans who found themselves in extrordaniary situations. Matheson's ground-breaking work helped lay the ground for others who came after him. His influence on Stephen King cannot be underestimated. As King says in *On Writing* (2000) "Richard Matheson was the author who influenced me most as a writer".

After publishing two crime novels in 1953 (*Someone is Bleeding* and *Fury on Sunday*), Matheson wrote his first horror novel *I Am Legend*. Ostensibly a vampire novel, it wasn't the first time Matheson used the vampire in a piece of fiction, nor would it be the last. Written during a period when he was working a full-time job and newly married with an infant son, *I Am Legend* depicts a lone man, Robert Neville, who is the survivor of a world-wide pandemic that has turned the world's population into vampiric creatures. Neville's daily life in suburban Los Angeles includes fortifying his house, collecting food as well as crucifixes, garlic, and other amulets of protection. *I Am Legend* proved to be extremely influential in not only vampire fiction, but in the development of the zombie in horror fiction.

(As an aside, the author's son, screenwriter Richard Christian Matheson, has told me that all of his father's short fiction and most of his novels were written on spec—i.e., with no contract or advance payment for publication. What should this tell those of you who are just starting out in this business? Follow your muse; write the kind of story you want to write).

Richard Matheson wasn't the only writer who was fusing the genres of science-fiction and horror in the early 1950s. There was also Robert Bloch, Eric Frank Russell, Robert Sheckly, Ray Bradbury, and several new writers who were bursting on the scene. However, while there was plenty of science-fiction/horror mashups going on in the pulps and on film (*War of the Worlds, The Thing From Another World*), it was in the world of comic books that the genres were gaining a huge foothold.

Comic books were nothing new by 1950. They'd been around since the late 1930s. Comic books grew out of the comic strips that were published in newspapers, with early titles consisting of reprints of some of the more popular newspaper comic strips. Eventually comic book writers and artists developed new characters and story-lines, with super heroes quickly becoming the most popular among readers. Early issues of all of the superhero comic books now command incredible prices on the secondary market (the famous issue of *Action Comics #1* featuring the first appearance of Superman has sold for three million bucks at auction in recent weeks).

Some of the early superheroes in comic books were occult in nature—*Black Widow, The Spector, Dr. Fate*. In 1946 the first comic book of illustrated horror fiction, *Eerie*, was published from Avon Books. It would set the tone for others that came along in the late 1940's—*Adventures into the Unknown* (which featured contributions from *Weird Tales* writers Frank Belknap Long and Manly Wade Wellman), *Journey Into Mystery* and the most infamous of all—the EC Comics horror titles.

ECs horror titles evolved from their comic *Crime Patrol*. Beginning in 1949, a horror story would be featured in each issue of *Crime Patrol* that was presented by a new character, the Crypt Keeper. This proved immensely popular, so EC publisher William Gaines launched seven titles in 1950, dubbing their release a "new trend" in comics. These seven releases, included three horror titles (*Tales From the Crypt*, *The Vault of Horror*, and *The Haunt of Fear*), two science-fiction titles (*Weird-Science, Weird-Fantasy*), crime fiction (*Crime SuspenStories* which had morphed from the earlier *Crime Patrol* title) and *Two Fisted Tales* (consisting of war stories). A few years later another crime publication would be added—*Shock SuspenStories*.

Die-hard horror aficionados of course know of EC's horror flagship titles, but they probably aren't as well versed in *Weird Science* or *Weird Fantasy*. That's a shame because there are some great tales of horror to be found in the pages of EC's science-fiction titles; it could also be found in the crime titles as well. Stories published in the EC comics line were unlike anything that had been published before in comics. Twist endings were plentiful. Grand Guignol was also present, with characters being stabbed, axed, ripped open, put through shredders, devoured, and eviscerated in great detail, often illustrated with bright, garish color. Traditional monsters like vampires, werewolves, and mummies were ghastly. Every few issue would be a horror-tinged retelling of a classic fairy tale called "Grim Fairy Tale". The EC horror comics were the 1950s version of the weird-menace pulps without the sex. Even the science-fiction stories that strayed into horror territory were gruesome.

Ray Bradbury had achieved fame as a science-fiction writer and EC adapted some of his most well-known stories for *Weird Science* and *Weird Fantasy*. However, it was the adaptation of his horror stories that won 1950s-era kids over in *Tales From the Crypt* and *The Vault of Horror*.

As a result of ECs success, other comic book publishers were quick to capitalize on their own brand of horror and they issued titles such as *Weird Horrors, Strange Tales, Web of Mystery, Tomb of Terror*, and *Journey into Fear*. By 1955 the Comics Code had been established by the industry as a result of mass hysteria (similar to the mass hysteria that greeted the weird-menace pulps some sixteen years earlier). Authority figures and misguided parents believed the EC Comics and their imitators were inspiring a rash of juvenile crime and delinquency. As a result, among the new rules established by the code, comic books could no longer use the words "horror," "terror" or "weird," and content had to be radically toned down. Thus ended the EC Horror and Science Fiction lines, and as we can see sixty years later, crime was eradicated from society.

By this time the pulp fiction magazines were dying a slow death. Most of those that survived up until 1954 had changed to digest size. *Weird Tales*, which had been slogging along under the editorship of Dorothy McIlwraith, was in a precarious position. Its sister magazine, *Short Stories*, was doing much better financially. McIlwraith had to make do with smaller budgets every year, forcing her to rely on reprints for a large part of the contents. Despite this, she managed to publish early stories by Joseph Payne Brennan and Richard Matheson along with the occasional tale from the magazine's old guard (Manly Wade Wellman, Robert Bloch, Mary Elizabeth Counselman). The September 1953 issue saw the magazine switch to digest size in an attempt to compete with the newer fantasy magazines crowding the fiction section on the magazine racks. The last issue was dated September 1954.

While the death of *Weird Tales* seems to signify a dearth in quality horror fiction in the 1950s, this cannot be further from the truth. The aforementioned *Magazine of Fantasy and Science Fiction* had been publishing high quality dark fantasy and horror stories since its inception in 1949. Other digest-sized magazines, most of them focused on science-fiction, also featured it—*Galaxy, Fantasy Fiction, Startling Stories*. Two of the best magazines that published horror and fantasy in the 1950s were *Fantastic* and *Beyond Fantasy Fiction*. Launched in 1952 by Ziff-Davis as a fantasy companion to *Amazing Stories, Fantastic* featured original fiction from the likes of Robert Bloch and Ray Bradbury as well as Richard Matheson and other new writers. *Beyond* only published ten issues from 1953 to 1955, but it published very good material by Richard Matheson, John Wyndham, Ray Bradbury, and Phillip K. Dick.

Throughout the 1950s the older pulp magazines were dead, but they hadn't really gone away—they'd merely changed format to digest size and continued. Four of these digest-sized magazines are still being published today (*Ellery Queen Mystery Magazine, Alfred Hitchcock's Mystery Magazine, The Magazine of Fantasy and Science Fiction*, and *Astounding*—now known as *Analog*). Fanzines were still being produced. Some of the finest stories of horror and dark fantasy, however, weren't being published in the pulps in the 1950s—they were being published in the slicks... and they were appearing in men's magazines.

When one thinks of the term "men's magazine" they probably think of *Esquire* these days. *Esquire* was around back then (its been around since 1933 and occasionally published horror and science fiction), but the men's magazines I'm referring to were more commonly called "pinup magazines" prior to 1950. Most specifically, they were porno magazines.

These magazines had been around in one form or another for decades. Due to various obscenity laws, they were most commonly available at specialty shops or resigned to special sections of the magazine rack. The photos found in these magazines would be considered softporn today, but were considered shocking and risqué for their times. However, in 1953 an enterprising young magazine publisher (and *Weird Tales* fan) aimed to change that.

Hugh Hefner started *Playboy* magazine with $8,000. The first issue featured Marilyn Monroe on the cover and was dated December 1953. Hefner wanted *Playboy* to appeal to middle-class and educated men, so in addition to the usual photographs and centerfolds of nude women, every issue featured interviews with various public figures as well as high-quality journalism covering a wide range of subjects. The magazine also featured fiction—and from the beginning, *Playboy* published very high quality stories of science-fiction and horror.

Among the writers to appear in the pages of *Playboy* throughout the 1950s was Robert Bloch, Ray Bradbury, Richard Matheson, Chad Oliver, Arthur C. Clarke, Jack

Finney, Henry Sleasar, Fredric Brown, Ray Russell, (who would become *Playboy's* fiction editor) and dozens of others. One of the magazine's earliest coup's was showcasing the brilliant work of Charles Beaumont.

Charles Beaumont's first published story was "The Devil, You Say?" in the January 1951 issue of *Amazing Stories.* Almost a dozen other stories followed in various digest-sized pulps until *Playboy* published "Black Country" in their September 1954 issue—the first original short story to be published by the magazine (Ray Bradbury's novel *Fahrenheit 451* was serialized by the magazine from March–May of that year). While Beaumont would make more sales to other digest-sized pulps, *Playboy* became one of his biggest markets. His work was so well-received by the magazine's readership that *Playboy* had first refusal rights to all of his short fiction. Probably his most notorious story to appear in the magazine was "The Crooked Man," a story that still resonates today. In it, the main character, a straight man, slips into a bar to meet with his female lover, hoping to escape detection. The setting of the story is an inverted United States, one in which being homosexual is the standard and heterosexuals are persecuted and forced to undergo "conversion therapy". Pretty heavy stuff for the mid-fifties. Readers were outraged, prompting Hugh Hefner to respond, "If it was wrong to persecute heterosexuals in a homosexual society then the reverse was wrong too." Beaumont later adapted some of his short fiction into well-known episodes of *The Twilight Zone.*

Are The Pulps Really Dead?

Finally after much promising, I'm going to venture into the world of pulps. After initially informing you that my next few columns were going to be on this subject, I'd find something new and more exciting to talk about. In that tradition of distraction, this column was originally intended to be about the Jeffrey Dahmer comic book, and the controversies it has caused. A phone conversation with Mike Baker got me on the track to focus on this, and upon receiving the latest AFRAID, I saw that the Mondo Cool Next Issue Box advertised me as finally getting to this much promised topic. That means I have to quit stalling and do it. Now.

Not that I don't think the pulps are interesting; they are, but I become easily distracted with the serial killing subjects, and if there's one thing I love delving into, it's the minds and doings of murderous psychopaths. The Dahmer comic is just an extension of that. I'll get into it in the near future. Promise.

On to the topic at hand.

The genesis for this topic originally sprang to mind two years ago at the HWA Convention in Redondo Beach. A huge caravan of us wound up going to lunch at an oceanside restaurant overlooking the beautiful Redondo Beach pier. If memory serves correctly, I believe the attendees at this luncheon included William Relling, Tom Elliott, Buddy Martinez, Terry Black, Mike Baker, Chris Lacher, Hugh B. Cave and I think Doug Clegg. And me, of course. There were more people at this lunch whom I can't recall, and the reason I remember this is because our table numbered at least fifteen, expanded from a group which originally consisted of five. Those of you who attend these things regularly know how hard it is to resist joining others for lunch.

I sat at one end of the table, with Chris Lacher on my right and Hugh and his charming wife Peggy on my left. As most writers do at these gatherings, we talked about writing. During the course of the conversation, Hugh remarked something to the effect of "It's really too bad that the pulps are gone, because young writer's like yourselves would have literally hundreds of markets available to you to sell your work." Chris said something to the effect that the pulps just changed form; they had essentially become the small press. Hugh only partially agreed with him. The small press displayed the same love and energy for the fields the way the pulps did, but most were a labor of love rather than one of profit. The audience for the small press was minimal compared to the audience for the pulps, which numbered in the thousands. We spent the rest of lunch talking about the pulps; or rather Chris and I listened as Hugh shared his memories on what it was really like writing for those magazines we've long heard or read about. And as Hugh reminisced on how times were for writers back in the pulp heydey, I realized that he was right. But only to a certain degree.

The pulps of the thirties and forties are gone, as are the benefits of writing for them. That much is certainly true.

But the pulps have never really, truly died.

Next time you walk into a bookstore, take a gander at the fiction shelves. Every catagory, from Mainstream to Romance to Science Fiction to Men's Adventure, has books which are no more than pulp material. Written for the sole purpose of entertainment, these are the books that nobody ever admits to buying. But somebody has got to be buying them, otherwise why would the publisher still be churning them out? Harlequin Romances are nothing but throwbacks to pulp magazines like Love Stories, Romance and True Love. Ditto action adventure novels and their resemblance to Doc Savage and Adventure. Argosy published tales of adventure on the high seas, the jungles of Africa, and the Orient. Mass market paperback publishers churn out the same kind of thing, usually with the same garish covers. Science Fiction and Fantasy sagas now come in the form of trilogies and Star Trek-related novels. Weird menace pulps like Spicy Mystery Stories and Black Mask are shrouded in the form of caper whodunnits. And of course, Weird Tales is still around, and similar horror pulps like Strange Tales, Horror Stories and Terror Tales are more or less reincarnated in the form of all those Zebra, Pinnacle and Leisure books you see every month. Different reading format, same basic set of rules with regards to style and pacing; fast-paced, action-oriented, never boring or preachy or overly moralistic. In short, good solid story-telling.

With regards to horror, science fiction and fantasy, the small press is the closest thing to the pulp magazines we do have. The significant differences are that 1) small press magazines aren't readily available at newstands the way pulps were, and 2) small press magazines don't pay nearly as much as what the pulps were paying. The average rate for a story sold to a pulp was a penny a word. Most small press magazines pay half of that, others even less. If you take inflation into account over the last fifty-odd years, a pulp would have to be paying ten cents a word and up just to stay abreast of the economy. And what magazine besides PLAYBOY can afford that?

Taking that into context, Hugh's remark rings true. Back during the pulp explosion, it was possible for one to make a living selling stories to the pulps (although one had to make a typewriter smoke in order to do so). With nearly three hundred markets to choose from, pulp writers just had to pound them out, send them in, and wait for the money to come in. The pulps were relatively easy for beginners to crack, as well. Back then, anyone who wanted to be a writer would find little resistance in selling his or her work to the pulps for the first time. Once the pace was kept up, a career could be had. In that aspect, the pulp mentality of discovering and nurturing new talent is almost gone. Another item which rings true in Hugh's argument.

Because television has replaced pulps as the idiom for America's main form of story entertainment, the hundreds of magazines that once catered to the many facets of popular fiction has dwindled drastically. The only logical thing one would have done when the pulps died was to move to writing for TV, which many writers did (such as Richard Matheson, Charles Beaumont, and Robert Bloch).

But what of those who came along too late in the transition? Folks who started writing during the late '70s/early '80s small press explosion.

Unless you live in or near L.A., your chances of writing for TV are pretty slim. But if you do, and if you make a living writing for TV, you are, in a sense, writing for the same audience that the pulps were geared toward: the mass market living rooms of America. TV is just a different medium.

The argument against Hugh's statement stems not only from TV, but those paperbacks I was referring to just a minute ago. In a May 1988 interview in the much missed HORRORSTRUCK, David J. Schow asserts: "Well, folks, the pulp magazines are ever with us. They are called movie novelizations today. They are called series novels, TV tie-ins. They follow the basic set of rules for the pulps, that is, they're written extremely fast, under impossible deadlines, for writer-for-hire minimal money, usually from behind pseudonyms, and they're all generally done in one draft."

Ever see those Men's Adventure novels? You know, the ones with huge pastel numbers on the spines which over-shadow the titles? Most of those are written so fast, and are deadlined so tight, that the writers hacking them out literally spit them out in under a month (sadly, it also shows in most cases). There are at least eight ongoing Action-Adventure novels being published as this column is being drafted, and if you search through other fiction catagories, you'll find more series abound; YA, Romance, Science Fiction, Westerns, Historical epics—there's even three different porno series available for your carnal pleasures.

Taken in this light, David's assertion rings true. And if you look beyond paperbacks, you'll find more aplenty in the magazine racks. Ever see those True Detective magazines? How 'bout those soppy Romance magazines (TRUE STORIES is a good example). Ever pick up a copy of the World Weekly News at the supermarket counter? A write-up in *Writer's Digest* on WWN and the kind of material they are looking for said they were seeking fiction. Come on now, did you really think the Bat Boy and the horse-with-the-human-face was real?

More pulp material lurks in the realm of the sex magazines. Same set of rules in regards to pacing and action, only in this genre you need to get more wet. Easy money can be had by churning this out, and the availability of the markets to sell this stuff to is endless. The money can be good, and if you're worried about being typed as a writer of pornography, then what the hell do you think pseudonyms are for?

If the pulps are still with us in other forms, then why is the assumption that "the pulps are dead" still abound?

Granted, almost anyone with the ability to write and a so-so imagination can sell to the sex market. The same rules of submissions and rejections apply just as if you were submitting something to any other magazine. Same thing for some of the other fields (true confession, WWN). If you're just starting out in the field, you can forget about writing Mack Bolan sagas until you start selling your own novels. Most publishers require that you have published at least one novel elsewhere before they sign you on for a series. That defeats the purpose if you're trying to break into writing full-time. If you have an agent that has an "in" to a gig, that would be an ideal way to go. Lots of guys popped their cherries in publishing this way (Dave Schow and John Shirley are ones who instantly come to mind). But unless you have an "in" you might as well resolve yourself to concentrating on your own work, which is more important anyway. One shouldn't have to resort to pulp work unless it is absolutely necessary. Like when you really need the money.

So are the pulps really dead?

Yes... and no. They are dead in the sense that there is no longer a proliferation of editors weaning new talent in the pages of monthly and bi-monthly fiction magazines. One might argue for the small press as a viable option, but many small press magazines are too narrowly focused in the material they're looking for ("we only publish Dark Fantasy fiction under four thousand words in length that takes place at night, with absolutely no profanity, sex, vampires, ghosts, zombies, serial killers, werewolves, aliens, mother-in-laws or negative stereotyping of minorities or women allowed. And there must be a happy ending). But they are still alive in the form of television sitcoms and serials, novelizations, series novels, confession stories in magazines, and hype stories found in cheesy tabloids (did you know that scientific studies show that all visiting extra terrestrials are under three feet tall?). The times have changed, and the pulps have changed with them. Sadly, the easy accessibility to open markets and the artistic freedom that reigned with them are now all but gone.

No Limits: Exploring The History Of Splatterpunk And Extreme Horror

DATELINE, March 1, 1991

The scene: the first World Horror Convention, Nashville, TN. As co-guest of honor David J. Schow personalizes a hardcover copy of his second novel, *The Shaft*, to Charles L. Grant in the middle of a busy dealer's room, he idly tells him about his latest novel-in-progress. Charlie listens with great interest, and it's obvious the novel has found an eager future reader.

I sit back from my table in the dealer's room, marveling at this scene. Only three short years before, Charlie was one of the loudest and most vociferous of the so-called proponents of "Quiet Horror" who, through interviews and columns, took swipes at a new group of writers who had dubbed themselves splatterpunks, giving many readers and fans the impression there was an all-out war between the two camps.

If you were involved in the scene in any way as a reader or a fan, or as a publisher, editor, or writer, then you were likely aware that horror fiction back then was split between two seemingly divided camps—writers like Charlie, William F.

Nolan, Dennis Etchison, and Dean Koontz who championed the quiet, more traditional end of horror fiction and routinely demeaned the work of a newer crop of writers emerging in the field that had come up with a splashy name for themselves—splatterpunks. The core writers in the splatterpunk movement consisted of David J. Schow, the writing team of John Skipp and Craig Spector, and Richard Christian Matheson; other then-new writers like Joe R. Lansdale, Ray Garton, and Clive Barker also came under the splatterpunk umbrella. What set their work apart from what was currently being published in the field was not only their depiction of graphic violence and sex, but a rock-and-roll vibrancy in their prose, characters who seemed more vibrant and real to the sea of twenty-somethings who were reading them, and themes that often addressed social topics and taboo subjects head-on. As for happy endings, forget about it. It didn't always happen.

The movement gained a lot of attention and won thousands of fans over. Not everybody was impressed. The chief argument against splatterpunk then is the same that is heard today: gore for gore's sake, style over substance, characters most readers wouldn't care about. Readers quickly took sides, and the battle raged in letters published in genre publications like *Locus* and *Horrorstruck*, during panels at conventions like World Fantasy and NECON, and became gossip fodder.

However, the general audience for horror fiction was largely unaware of the movement until 1988 when two key essays examining splatterpunk were published—one in *Rod Serling's The Twilight Zone Magazine*, the other in *Midnight Graffiti*. As a young fan and wanna-be writer myself during that period, I immediately identified with the key figureheads of splatterpunk. I was familiar with their work already; seeing their photographs in the magazines was like seeing an alternate image of my friends and I. We shared the same cultural heritage. What wasn't there to like?

I was fortunate enough to meet them in August of 1988, at a book-signing in Pasadena, California. After the signing, we invited them to a party and we sat up all night, talking and drinking beer and generally having a good time.

Despite my youthful embrace of splatterpunk, I was also a fan and great admirer of writers like Charles L. Grant, Dennis Etchison, Stephen King, and Ramsey Campbell—the so-called 'old guard.' When my friend Buddy Martinez and I got involved in publishing, we knew we wanted to publish the kind of fiction we loved to read—horror fiction, in all its various sub-genres and styles. We didn't see what the fuss was in all the sniping and personal attacks being parried back and forth. So we decided to create a vehicle that would be a showcase for *all* forms of dark fiction. Thankfully, the splatterpunk guys were onboard with our plans. So were other writers. In fact, our most powerful supporters came from the more quiet side of the camp.

When I originally met Charlie Grant at the 1989 World Fantasy Convention I was expecting derision at my mention that I was publishing a brand new novella by Schow in the debut issue of *Iniquities*. Buddy and I resembled musicians in a metal band rather than magazine editors. In fact, we looked more like those splatterpunk guys than any NY editor. I thought Charlie would dismiss us with an air of snobbery. That wasn't the case at all. Charlie was funny, warm, sincere, caring, and very interested in our project. Best of all, despite his stature in the field, I detected the fan deep within him.

Charlie's paraphrased response: "It's important for a dark fiction magazine to represent all forms of horror fiction. Splatterpunk is an important part of the genre. It *should* be represented."

I was initially surprised by Charlie's comment. That surprise quickly turned to gratitude. It was a response that was quickly echoed by William F. Nolan and others of the old guard. Likewise, in the months that followed, as Buddy and I prepared the debut issue of our magazine, the core members of the splat pack echoed these sentiments to us during private conversations. As a young neophyte editor-publisher just getting a foothold in the field, I was expecting more of the derision and bickering I'd only read about when I was an outsider. Now that I was an active participant, I was seeing an entirely different view; I was witnessing mutual respect from the two camps for each other's work.

That mutual respect was demonstrated even further to me in 1993, when I had the singular honor of acting as ghost editor for *Book of the Dead 3*, which was being assembled by Craig Spector. Long story. One of the best stories received for the anthology was a contribution by Charlie Grant. It combined all the elements that made Charlie's work so celebrated, yet it was extremely twisted and managed to be subtle. Charlie expressed surprise at being asked to contribute to an anthology of flesh-eating zombie stories, commenting that he "doesn't write that sort of thing," but he handled the task admirably. *Book of the Dead 3* imploded, some of its contents appeared in the John Skipp assembled anthology *Mondo Zombie*. The Grant story wasn't among them. The story, to the best of my knowledge, remains unpublished.

I thought about this as I watched David and Charlie talk in that busy dealer's room. Charlie was marveling at the cover of *The Shaft*, which depicted a giant worm bearing needle sharp teeth from an oversize, dripping mouth. Charlie related that it reminded him of the covers of the British Nasties, which he claimed to be a big fan of and which I was aware of but not well versed in at the time. I later learned that the so-called Nasties were the UK's equivalent of the splatterpunk movement, and were the literary counter-part to the Video Nasties (Britain's pejorative for splatter films).

Flash forward ten years later and I buy a story by a guy I'd never heard of named Wrath James White, for an anthology I'm co-editing with Garret Peck called *Tooth and Claw*. Wrath's story came unsolicited over the transom, but it had all the elements I like in graphic fiction. It was visceral in all the right places. It was short and packed a hell of an emotional punch. Had Wrath emerged on the scene fifteen years earlier, he would have been lumped in with the splatterpunk movement, much like Ray Garton and Joe R. Lansdale were during that pivotal moment.

Wrath James White, however, became one of a number of writers who were part of something called Extreme Horror.

What the hell is that? Surely Extreme Horror, like the British Nasties, is just another name for Splatterpunk, right? Or is Extreme Horror something entirely different? As can be expected, there are numerous viewpoints. For many people, Extreme Horror is no different than splatterpunk. In fact, proponents of this view tend to use the more current term—Extreme Horror—to describe not only writers like Edward Lee and Wrath James White, but the splatterpunks.

Others, however, have an opposing view; Extreme Horror is simply a grosser and more extreme version of what constitutes modern horror fiction and has nothing to do with splatterpunk. Some even go further to say that it lacks the emotional intensity and the social commentary of splatterpunk. Not surprisingly, the writers of both schools have their own views.

"Extreme Horror grew out of the Splatterpunk revolution and just continued pushing the envelope so far that new writers are not even aware an envelope exists," Wrath James White tells me. "The boundaries are invisible now. What is called Extreme Horror today is so divorced from the mainstream that it is perhaps a bit out of control. The Splatterpunks of the late eighties and early nineties crossed the line deliberately and were therefore able to maximize the effect when they did it. Today, those lines are so lax and have been so obscured that most new writers don't know where they are. Honestly, I'm sort of a prime example of this. I still don't really know what is and is not acceptable. I'm still breaking rules that I'm completely unaware of."

The idea of horror fiction needing to be labeled as extreme may strike some as redundant. Say the word "horror" to the average person on the street and the most common theme you'll hear is a smattering of the following: "Horror fiction is bloody and violent, it's all about killing and murder." "Horror stories are all about slashers and psycho killers torturing women." "Horror is *Nightmare on Elm Street* and *Saw* and Stephen King." All of these statements are true to an extent. But if you're a reader of this magazine, you know horror fiction is much more than that. You know that horror fiction also encompasses the classic ghost story, tales of the supernatural,

SF/horror hybrids, the weird fiction of Clark Ashton Smith and Thomas Ligotti, the cosmic horror of H. P. Lovecraft and his imitators, the psychological thrillers of Robert Bloch and Jim Thompson. Go back even further and you'll come across the plays of John Webster and William Shakespeare, many which contained horrific elements and flirted with the supernatural.

Throughout its history, literature we now recognize as horror has always pushed the envelope. Witness *The Monk* by Matthew Gregory Lewis. This 1796 novel, written when the author was nineteen years old, was immediately banned for obscenity and blasphemy, was censored in later versions, and turned the concept of the gothic novel upside down. Lewis wanted to see how far he could go, and he did—he completely obliterated the gothic archetype already established by such figures as Ann Radcliffe and Horace Walpole, and earned the admiration of Lord Byron and the Marquis de Sade (who had shocked French authorities with the publication of *Justine* only a few short years before, and whose 1785 novel *The 120 Days of Sodom* would go unpublished until the early twentieth century). Other authors of the gothic novel were quick to hop on the trend, and the early 1800's saw a slew of imitators, many of them plagiarized versions of Lewis's masterpiece.

With that in mind, it can be argued that what we know and recognize as Extreme Horror is nothing new. It is simply fiction that pushes the artistic and literary aesthetics of its time.

The Penny Dreadfuls and the Dime Novels of the mid to late 1800's published fiction that was considered lurid (but wasn't really that extreme) for its time. These publications gave birth to the pulps in 1896. During this period, the traditional ghost story flourished, along with supernatural and ironic tales by such writers as Ambrose Bierce and Arthur Machen. The term "raw heads and bloody bones" type of fiction was a British pejorative during this period, and was used to differentiate the more genteel traditional ghost story from the more graphic horror tales that were beginning to emerge in this period, especially those written by Dick Donovan and Clive Pemberton. Indeed, Donovan's "The Cave of Blood" and "The Mystic Spell" are abound with full-fledged blood and gore, an excess that was very out of place for the late Victorian-era. This approach dovetailed with the emergence of the pulps in America, and was considered to be a conscious decision on the part of the writer to be lurid and vulgar. Most of the ghost story writers of this era did not write graphic horror of this type. Their approach was more subtle, an effort to "make your flesh creep". To resort to the "raw heads and bloody bones" type of graphic horror fiction that was gaining attention in the late Victorian period was, well, rather uncomely for those times.

This "raw heads and bloody bones" approach influenced writers that would appear in the pulps, particularly *Weird Tales* magazine. While *Weird Tales* is often not thought of today to have been a purveyor of graphic horror fiction, the material they published in the first fifteen years of its run certainly pushed the envelope of conventional tastes for its time. "The Loved Dead" by C.M. Eddy Jr. is rumored to have sparked such outrage in 1924 in its depiction of necrophilia, that its May/June 1924 in which the story appeared was removed from many newsstands. The magazine forged on, though, and published a number of stories in its three decade run that are now considered classics in the fields of fantasy, science fiction, and horror.

While supernatural horror was always a staple of *Weird Tales*, the occasional gruesome or cruel *tale* would creep into its pages. One such story, "The Copper Bowl" by George Fielding Eliot, appeared in a 1925 issue. In the story, the protagonist is tied to a table and a live rat is placed on his bare stomach and covered by a copper bowl; the copper bowl is then heated gradually. Guess what Mr. Rat will gnaw through to escape the heat if it becomes too much for him? Frank Belknap Long is more known today for his classic Lovecraftian tale "The Hounds of Tindalos," but he published a number of stories in *Weird Tales* (and in a 1930's era weird-menace pulp *Thrilling Mystery*) that were much more graphic and twisted than his pal Howie Lovecraft would ever pen. Likewise, a young writer named Robert Bloch published a handful of tales that pushed the envelope for those times ("Mannikins of Horror" from a 1939 issue of *Weird Tales* is a prime example; the idea for the 1982 Splatter film *Basket Case* could have been lifted from this story). There are other examples of tales with a similar streak in the annals of *Weird Tales*, but for the most part the magazine stuck with the more varied form of genre fiction and rarely published extremely graphic horror fiction.

It wasn't until a straight crime fiction pulp called *Dime Mystery Magazine* changed its editorial format in 1933 that things began to change. Heavily influenced by Grand Guignol theater in France, Popular Publications needed to boost sales of their floundering title and they succeeded with this new vision that would mimic the blood-drenched drama from the Grand Guignol. Within two years they'd added additional titles to their stable, most notably *Terror Tales* and *Horror Stories*. Other pulp publishers followed suit with their own titles, most notably *Thrilling Mystery* and *Uncanny Tales*; thus the "shudder pulps" or "weird menace" pulps were born.

The stories published in the weird menace pulps adhered to a basic formula: the protagonist was always pitted against evil or sadistic antagonists. The conflict always had to be bizarre with a strong suggestion of the supernatural. The atmosphere was always eerie, at times gothic in nature. Graphic scenes of torture and murder were always required. However, the stories had to be resolved with rational explanations. The story titles had to be dramatic and over-the-top. To wit: "Death Calls from the Madhouse". "The Dead Hate the Living," "They Thirst at Midnight" and my personal favorite—"The Molemen Want Your Eyes".

The cover art was what sold the magazines, though. Lovely scantily clad women being menaced by hunchbacks, mad scientists, gibbering apes and other fiends were the staple. The August 1937 issue of *Dime Mystery Magazine* depicted a bikini-clad lady about to be chopped in half by a mad scientist's assistant. One particular gruesome cover of *Horror Stories* depicted a man bearing a cat o'nine tails whipping his menagerie of scantily clad women while he sat cross-legged on a throne. The primary theme running through all the covers of the weird menace pulps was a sense of perverted menace with a hint of S&M. Indeed, for years, pulp collectors bought crumbling copies of the weird menace pulps based on the cover art alone.

With the notable exception of the work of Hugh B. Cave, for decades the stories that were published within their pages languished in relative obscurity. While it's true that most of the work that appeared in the shudder pulps just wasn't very good, there was some superior work being published within their pages that would rival the more popular *Weird Tales* writers. Thanks to the work of anthologists like John Pelan, the work of Wyatt Blassingame, John H. Knox, and Arthur J. Burks are now being reprinted and recognized as minor classics.

This formula of increased depiction of violence and sex made the shudder pulps very different from the standard genre pulps like *Weird Tales* and *Amazing Stories*. As the Great Depression wound on, the stories that appeared in their pages became more savage and violent. Stories like "Imp of Satan" by Hugh B. Cave and "The Molemen Want Your Eyes" by Frederick C. Davis contained scenes of sheer brutality and sexual imagery that went even beyond standard weird-menace fare. Considering decency standards in the 1930's, it was a minor miracle they were even published. By the late 1930's, there were no less than three-dozen weird-menace titles competing for rack space. Even *Weird Tales* got in on the action and introduced its own weird menace character, Dr. Satan.

In 1939 New York City Mayor Fiorello LaGuardia became appalled by one particular gruesome cover of *Horror Stories* and made noise about it. Within months the torture scenes disappeared from the covers. The women gained clothing. And the fiction became less controversial. By the early 1940's, the shudder pulps had either reformed or disappeared entirely from the newsstands.

As the pulps died and the paperback boom began, horror fiction went through its many twists and turns in the field.

Through it all, the occasional novel or short story was published that seemed to be starkly different in terms of its extreme nature. *Echo of a Curse* by R. R. Ryan (published in 1940), despite its seemingly quiet nature and slow and dreadful buildup, contains elements of cruelty and perversity usually found in a modern day Edward Lee novel. *House of Flesh* by Bruno Fischer was a 1951 Gold Medal paperback original that could have been written during the heyday of the shudder pulps (Fischer wrote a slew of material for the shudder pulps). *Some of Your Blood* by Theodore Sturgeon (1962) contains gruesome scenes of bloodletting that were shocking in their day. Anthony Burgess' *A Clockwork Orange* (1962) was explicit in its depiction of gang violence; its off-the-wall excess continues to inspire and outrage to this day. British anthologist Charles Birkin published a series of short stories in the mid 1960's that are noted for their unrestrained scenes of cruelty ("A Lovely Bunch of Coconuts," "Waiting for Trains").

While graphic horror fiction seemed to disappear from prose and the pulps, it flourished in an entirely brand new medium: comic books.

While not the first comic book company to publish graphic horror in their pages, the EC line of horror comics—*The Vault of Horror*, *The Haunt of Fear*, and *Tales from the Crypt*—are the best examples of where graphic horror could be found during this period. Graphic horror fiction wasn't only evident in the company's horror comics; it could also be found sprinkled in their two science fiction titles (*Weird Science* and *Weird Fantasy*) and in their crime story comics (*Shock SuspenseStories* and *Crime SuspenseStories*). The EC-line of comics are memorable for their ghoulish and visceral story-telling and art. One *Vault of Horror* story ended on a baseball field, with the strung-out intestines of the hapless villain tracing the line between home plate and third base. Other stories included gruesome decapitations, dismemberments, disembowelments and other horrific finales, all with some kind of moral judgment at the end. Parents complained, government officials began to take note, and when a 1954 issue of *Crime SuspenseStories* depicted a woman's severed head held by her long hair by her faceless male killer (bearing an axe), the howls of protest grew louder. Senate hearings resulted in the formation of The Comics Code, which all but ended EC Publications' empire and killed dozens of imitators. All of this is detailed in the must-read volume *The Ten Cent Plague: The Great Comic Book Scare and How It Changed America* (David Hajdu, Farrar, Straus and Giroux, 2008).

With the exception of comic books until the dreaded Code came along, there wasn't a whole lot of extreme horror being published.

The real-life horrors of World War II and the Korean and Vietnam Wars may have played into this. Readers desiring escapism from the Great Depression could let their imaginations be taken away by the extreme stories in the shudder pulps. But the horrors of World War II and the impending Cold War had a psychological effect on readers and many writers. Our fears were internalized; we were no longer afraid of the financial uncertainty the Great Depression brought to our collective psyches, which evolved into many of the plot excesses of the weird menace authors (overcoming incredible and at times horrifying odds to survive and save the heroine from the clutches of a hideous monster). Our fears were now global; the threat of Communism (which gave birth to classics like *The Body Snatchers* by Jack Finney); the threat of nuclear annihilation (pick any 1950's SF/Horror film). Through it all, western society was changing rapidly. In the US, the middle-class was growing; people were moving into the suburbs. Writers like Ray Bradbury, Richard Matheson, and Robert Bloch capitalized on this. And as the 1950's became the 1960's and we began to look at our neighbor with a shade of suspicion and distrust, something else was happening in the world of film.

Always popular, horror films had evolved from cinema's early days as a medium to adapt classic works of horror and dark fantasy, to vehicles of mining the fears of alien invasion and killer beasts. In 1963 Hershel Gordon Lewis upped the ante with *Blood Feast*, which became notorious for its scenes of explicit blood, gore, and violence. Thus, the splatter film was born.

Early splatter films emphasized elaborate special effects over characterization and plot. At times, the gore scenes were so over-the-top they produced laughter instead of revulsion. One early exception to this was George A. Romero's *Night of the Living Dead* (1968). This stark black and white film hit on all six cylinders in terms of plot, pacing, characterization, mood, theme, and gore. As the 1970's dawned, depictions of violence in film became more prevalent with the loosening of censorship laws governing film and books. Films like Wes Craven's *The Last House on the Left* and Alejandro Jodorowsky's *El Topo* (1970) gave way to a slew of imitators that played the Drive-Ins and grindhouse theaters of America. Even films with larger budgets began upping the ante on their depictions of sex and violence—*Deliverance, Straw*

Dogs, The Exorcist, Jaws, and *Carrie.* It was inevitable that prose writers would follow.

Looking back, it is difficult to discern where the demarcation point for extreme horror began prior to the death of the shudder pulps. With a handful of exceptions, nothing the modern reader would label as extreme horror was published in this period. Stephen King's debut novel *Carrie* certainly contained graphic scenes of impalement, and his follow-up, *'Salem's Lot* contained a scene even more gruesome than its predecessor (and this scene was toned down from its original first draft at the request of King's editor at the time). The 1974 Mendal W. Johnson novel *Let's Go Play at the Adams'* pre-dated the classic Jack Ketchum novel *The Girl Next Door* by fifteen years with an ending that *wasn't* happy and that made more than a few readers throw the book across the room in disgust. James Herbert's first novel, *The Rats,* published in 1974, was a grim, sadistic tale of mutant rats overrunning London and eating the human population. These novels were anomalies though; modern horror fiction became extremely popular with the general reading public in this period due to the enormous success of Ira Levin and William Peter Blatty, and by the end of the 1970's, writers like Stephen King, Peter Straub, Charles L. Grant, John Coyne, and Ramsey Campbell became more or less integrated as mainstream fiction.

It was at this point that horror began to spawn mutations.

In 1980 a paperback original called *The Cellar* by Richard Laymon was published. It was so over-the-top, so brutal in its very spare prose and its depictions of graphic violence, that it was an immediate hit and gave the author a strong underground cult following. The following year, another relatively unknown writer named Jack Ketchum made a similar debut with a paperback original called *Off Season*. This bare bones narrative of a group of friends menaced by a large family of inbred cannibals along the coastal Maine woods was also a hit. Both authors produced further works, each of them unique in their voice and their brutal form of narrative. Their works were stark contrasts to what was currently being published and embraced in the rather insular world of horror fiction, which by then had grown up and become a marketing category in publishing seemingly overnight.

Prior to 1980 or so, mass market publishers did not market dark fiction as horror. Genres like Romance, Mystery, and Science Fiction had existed as marketing labels for decades, but prior to Stephen King's success, horror fiction was usually lumped in with Science Fiction or was simply published as mainstream fiction. By 1983, things had changed. All of a sudden bookstores had horror sections, just like they did for Science Fiction and Romance. The success of Stephen King and Peter Straub was infectious and other writers wanted in on it.

Thus the great horror boom in mass-market publishing began. Long dominated by the successful template established with *Rosemary's Baby* and *The Exorcist*, most horror fiction was suburban in its setting, middle-class in character, its terrors solidly rooted in conformity, about external forces intruding into everyday life. This form of horror fiction became very traditional in its form and gained a degree of mainstream respectability.

It was during this time that Richard Laymon and Jack Ketchum continued to quietly produce well-crafted novels that pushed the aesthetics of commercial horror fiction (they were joined rather briefly in 1982 by a writer normally known for his Science Fiction, John Shirley, with an incredibly brutal novel called *Cellars*). And it was also during this time when a diverse group of writers began to publish short fiction that was daring and raw in its depiction of sex and violence. Their fiction was set not in the suburbs, but in the inner city streets and back alleys of big cities.

By 1986 a core group of this new pack of writers had a catchy name for themselves. Splatterpunks.

The very word came about as a joke. At the 1986 World Fantasy Convention a group of writers including David J. Schow, John Skipp, and Craig Spector were sitting around the hotel bar talking about how their work, as well as the works of other new writers like Clive Barker (then riding high on *The Books of Blood* and *The Damnation Game*) and Joe R. Lansdale (then gaining attention with his powerful short fiction) seemed to be shaking things up in the field. John Skipp and Craig Spector's debut novel, *The Light at the End*, had taken off in sales and David J. Schow's powerful short fiction was making editors and readers sit up and take notice. As John Skipp would later say: "The common thread that bound our works together was universal: depicting scenes of unflinching violence, often in more elaborate and colorful ways than our predecessors; depicting scenes of very honest, sometimes weird, and sometimes disturbing sex; and a sense of cultural subversiveness that was far from anything found in mainstream horror fiction."

"It was one of those things where you're sitting around a hotel bar at a convention just talking," Craig Spector recounts to me. "There was the cyberpunk movement in SF, and somebody said, 'We better come up with a name for what we're doing before somebody else does', so we were just going back and forth making shit up, all the names ending in the word 'punk' and it was getting kinda ridiculous. And then David J. Schow said 'splatterpunk' and everybody at our table stopped talking. We all knew instinctively that this was what we should call ourselves."

John Skipp: "We all laughed and fifteen minutes later, it was all over the convention."

As Richard Christian Matheson would reflect to me recently: "It was clearly a marketing ploy, a gimmick. The four of us shared a sense of camaraderie. My fiction was very different than theirs (Schow, Skipp & Spector) and I wasn't really into the excessiveness as much as they were, but we all shared certain aesthetics in our work. In fact, I commented in an interview we did for *Penthouse* on splatterpunk that said something to the effect of 'If their work is the scalpel that opens the wound, I'm the needle that injects the virus'."

Within months, convention panels had Loud vs. Quiet horror debates. The old guard quickly established itself as being voraciously against this seemingly dangerous new trend in fiction. Some writers were lumped in with the splatter-punks (Ray Garton, Robert McCammon, and Joe R. Lansdale). Aside from their artistic aesthetics and their average age, much of what bound their work together was a sort of hip sense of fashion and music in the 1980's. Matheson, Schow, and Skipp and Spector, resembled guys in a rock band more than they did writers, and the tone of their work was urbane, hip, their prose pedal-to-the-metal and crackling with a kind of back-beat rock and roll fusion. Film was another huge influence. From the 1968 George Romero classic *Night of the Living Dead*, to the Italian horror of Fulci and Argento, to the 1970's grindhouse gore films, film became a more overt influence on splatterpunk than the gothic backdrops of classic horror fiction. This is evident from the vivid, almost cinematic scenes, the crackling intensity of the prose. As David J. Schow would tell the *New York Times* in a March 1991 article on splatterpunk, "It's not enough to see the shadow behind the door—people want to see what's making the shadow, what it looks like and how it comes apart."

That's not to say the writers grouped under the splatterpunk umbrella were not influenced by traditional horror fiction; they very much were. Robert Bloch, Gerald Kersh, Fritz Leiber, Harlan Ellison, John Brunner, Ray Bradbury, Charles Beaumont, Richard Matheson—all of them were influential to a degree.

And while the core writers who embraced the splatterpunk label, those who were lumped in with the movement have varying views on it. Joe R. Lansdale never really saw himself as a splatterpunk. Ray Garton's early work, while containing several scenes and situations of extreme violence, was actually more rooted in the traditional horror of the Stephen King mode. Clive Barker's early work was harsh, raw, with that sustained edge so prevalent found in the splatterpunk writing, but he quickly shifted his style to concentrate on big sprawling novels of urban fantasy with horrific elements, something he called *fantastique*.

Splatterpunk made a huge impact in publishing in ways many of its most ardent supporters never could have imagined. "When we started," Craig Spector says, "what bound us and our work together was a sense of culture. Splatterpunk was very tribal. It was depraved fiction for depraved times. We were born and came of age during the height of communism, McCarthyism, the civil rights movement, the birth of rock and roll, Vietnam, the turbulent sixties and early seventies and we absorbed this stuff as kids. And as the seventies gave way to the eighties and the culture changed, became more depraved and decadent, our work reflected that. We just seemed to come on the scene at the right time. It was the perfect storm in terms of culture, the publishing industry, and the current state of horror fiction at the time. It was time for the next big thing to happen in horror and we were it."

As splatterpunk became popular, various small and semi-pro publications were launched, influenced by this new wave of cutting edge horror fiction. Some of the more notable ones included *Grue*, published out of New York, which published notable work by Wayne Allen Sallee ("Rapid Transit") and Joe R. Lansdale ("God of the Razor"), and *New Blood*, published out of Glendora, California, which published original fiction by Richard Laymon and Graham Masterton. I hasten to add that my own publication, *Iniquities*, was also part of this pack of magazines launched during this period.

Ironically, the splatterpunk school of writers were active around the time the British "Nasties" school of writers were reaching their commercial peak across the pond: James Herbert, Graham Masterton, Shaun Hutson, Guy N. Smith, and John Brosnam (well-known to horror fans as Harry Adam Knight). Drawing on the same cultural and pop culture influences as the state-side splatterpunks, this diverse group of writers had a more developed following in the UK. The success of the early works of Shaun Hutson led Ramsey Campbell to dismiss Hutson's work with an air of disdain in the British genre press. Despite this, Hutson's work was hugely popular in the late 1980's and his novels contained incredibly gross scenes of violence. The novels of Graham

Masterton during this period also displayed a sense of hyper-violence not found in his later works (the publication of his short story "Eric the Pie" in the UK horror magazine *Frighteners* caused such outrage that it effectively killed UK distribution for the periodical, leading to its demise). Needless to say, American authors of hardcore horror found rabid followings in England. Richard Laymon achieved more success there than in his home country; the works of David J. Schow, Joe R. Lansdale, Ray Garton, and Skipp and Spector all found receptive readers in the UK and the rest of Europe.

By 1989 splatterpunk was the proverbial topic in magazine columns and convention panels. The most repeated criticism of splatterpunk was the one frequently made against graphic horror films—the lack of characters the reader could identify and care about. Another complaint was the emphasis of gore and violence over the story arc. It was these complaints that caused many to dismiss the works produced by the splatterpunks without actually reading their work.

What was never mentioned was that the writers commonly associated with splatterpunk were capable of producing exceptional quiet works as well. David J. Schow's "Red Light" won a World Fantasy Award in the short fiction category in 1987, a tale which has a slow, atmospheric build and could have easily fit in with Charles L. Grant's award-winning *Shadows* anthologies. Richard Christian Matheson, Joe R. Lansdale, Robert R. McCammon, and Richard Laymon all produced versatile works ranging from strange surrealism to traditional hardboiled crime to whimsical fantasy in the *Twilight Zone* mode. Even the writing team of John Skipp & Craig Spector, who often bore the brunt of the harsh criticism toward splatterpunk, were capable of producing quieter and sustained shorter works to great success.

It is the general consensus of the core-group of authors most commonly associated with splatterpunk that the "movement" died due to the tremendous sea-change that began to occur with mass-market publishing in the early nineties. The horror-boom of the 1980's produced hundreds of novels from every mass-market publisher, with some houses publishing four horror novels a month. With such an over-saturation of horror novels in the marketplace, readers got burned out, especially when much of the work being published was rubbish. One of the other contributing factors to the movement's death was the general misconception of what splatterpunk really was, as evidenced in Paul M. Sammon's introduction to the anthology *Splatterpunks: Extreme Horror* (St. Martin's Press, 1990).

Content-wise, *Splatterpunks: Extreme Horror* was a solid anthology containing mostly reprints by a wide range of writers. Curiously absent from the anthology were the works of David J. Schow and the writing team of Skipp and Spector (John Skipp was represented by a solo effort, "Film At Eleven"). As Craig Spector explains it: "Paul Sammon's definition of splatterpunk, which was an attempt to define it in academic terms, centered mostly on the depiction of graphic sex and violence and did not address the social issues we were tackling in our work. It was also filled with quotes from writers like Joe Lansdale saying they weren't splatterpunks. It didn't really penetrate the deep issues that defined the work. At the same time, he (Sammon) was identifying himself as a splatterpunk, when he really wasn't."

Sammon followed up *Splatterpunks: Extreme Horror* with *Splatterpunks II: Over the Edge* in 1995, another mostly reprint anthology featuring works by Brian Hodge, Robert Devereaux, Poppy Z. Brite, Christa Faust, and others. Schow has commented that the female writers that came of age during this period (The Riot Grrls of Horror) can be seen as a splat pack II of the female persuasion—Caitlen R. Kiernan, Yvonne Navarro, Kathe Koja, Christa Faust, Lucy Taylor, Poppy Z. Brite. While Faust openly admits that the splatterpunk writers were an early influence, Poppy Z. Brite has acknowledged Stephen King and Ramsey Campbell as her primary influences. Another less obvious influence is the fiction of Dennis Cooper, most specifically *Frisk* (1991), an extremely sexually explicit and violent novel about a gay man's obsession with the dead that predates Brite's own *Exquisite Corpse.* Dennis Cooper's work flew under the radar of most devotees of graphic horror fiction, but Brite was an early admirer of his fiction.

By 1994 splatterpunk as a marketing ploy was dead. The writing team of Skipp and Spector broke up, with Spector finding work in film and producing two solo novels—*To Bury the Dead* and *Underground*—and Skipp moving to solo projects, culminating in several solo and collaborative pieces with Marc Levinthal (most notably, the collaborative novel *The Emerald Burrito of Oz*); he continues to produce quality work today, some of it in collaboration with Cody Goodfellow (*Jake's Wake*). David J. Schow became a successful scriptwriter (*The Crow*, Showtime's *The Hunger* and *Masters of Horror* series) and continues to turn out powerful short stories and novels. Richard Christian Matheson published his debut novel *Created By* and continues working in film and

TV; a definitive collection of his powerful short fiction, *Dystopia*, was published in 2000. The horror boom in publishing was over, the distribution method for books changed drastically, and much of the good horror fiction being published appeared in the small press or from NY houses as mainstream or crime fiction.

Splatterpunk may have been dead with mainstream publishing, but its spirit was very much alive in the pages of small press magazines. *Grue* was still around, but published infrequently. Others had gone belly-up while new ones sprang up to take their place. Some of the more notable ones included publications like *Wicked Mystic, Aberrations*, and *Into the Darkness* that published work by Gerard Houarner, Lucy Taylor, and Edward Lee. In 1993, an enterprising small press publisher and writer named John Pelan started Silver Salamander Press and issued Lucy Taylor's first collection, *The Flesh Artist*. Comparisons to Clive Barker's *Books of Blood* were quick to follow. Pelan followed this collection with other volumes by a wide range of writers (Adam Troy Castro, Michael Shea) while elsewhere, in Florida, another small publisher began tapping the same vein.

In 1995 Necro Press published a 500-copy chapbook by Edward Lee called *Header*. No stranger to depicting graphic scenes of violence in his work as a novelist, Lee had been on the scene for a number of years, quietly writing paperback originals for houses like Zebra and Onyx/Berkley. "In the early 90's I wrote (can't remember the order!) *Header* and *The Bighead*, essentially as experiments that I didn't think would get published in a million years," Lee tells me. "I was doing it for fun. Around this same time, I'd been turned on to Dave Barnett's magazine *Into the Darkness*, and he published one of my stories ("The Wrong Guy"), which I'd written just for a fun experiment (comedic horror smut). I told Dave about *Header* and *The Bighead* and he expressed interest after reading them (I was scarcely even aware of the extent of the cult horror market at that time) and he published them, to my flabbergasted surprise."

Header is essentially a graphic tale of family revenge. What sets it apart from his earlier work is the unflinching perversity in the depiction of exactly what a header is (and if you don't know what it is, I'm not telling you).

Lee followed this up with *Goon*, a collaborative effort with John Pelan, which started as a solo piece for an anthology of wrestling stories Pelan was assembling: "I asked John to look at it and he offered to re-write the ending and even said he could sell it with no trouble. I kind of laughed, thinking, 'I doubt anyone would publish it because one, it's too scatological and two, it's about wrestling.'"

They sent it to Necro Publications where it was promptly rejected as being too extreme. John recounts: "I called Dave Barnett and said, 'what do you mean it's too extreme? You're the king of hardcore horror, if you don't publish *Goon*, you'll be a pussy'. Dave didn't want to be known as a pussy, so he published it."

This prepared Lee's new fan base for his next project and, some say, his masterpiece in the field of extreme horror: *The Bighead*. Lee produced further works in this vein, in which he continuously pushed the limits in the depiction of grotesque violence and perverse sex (and some say, bad taste): *The Pig, Ever Nat, The Teratologist* (with Wrath James White), and *The House*, among others.

A decade after the birth of splatterpunk, the critics of this new extreme horror movement were even quicker to condemn this new trend. Darrel Schweitzer described a reading at a World Horror Convention in Weird Tales that "...went for the gross-out as much as possible—in fact to a degree seldom seen in legally circulated literature. Well, fine. This is all very amusing, even as small boys amuse themselves at camp with disgusting stories told in the dark. But that direction seems to me a dead end. It's a great way to sell about four hundred copies in an expensive, limited edition and no more."

The criticism didn't affect those who were producing this new blend of extreme horror. "Basically, we had a blast writing this stuff," John Pelan says. "It was for fun. It wasn't meant to be serious at all." The writing team of Edward Lee and John Pelan produced a number of collaborative efforts (*Splatterspunk: The Micah Hayes Stories, Family Tradition*) and Lee produced several solo works that exceeded the depiction of violence and perversity of *The Bighead* and *The Pig*.

Lee and Pelan's efforts were hugely successful, and spawned the legendary Gross-Out Contest tournaments at the World Horror Convention (which, ironically, had spun off five or six years before from the World Fantasy Convention, with David J. Schow and the Skipp & Spector team as their inaugural guests of honor).

Edward Lee and John Pelan quickly became associated as writers of hardcore horror (despite each author's talent in excelling at other forms of fiction). This label has stuck with readers so much that those who first encounter Edward Lee's work in the small press and give his mass-market novels a try (published by Leisure Books) come away disappointed. "It became obvious to me very quickly," Edward Lee says, "That a good many readers who started off reading my hardcore material *hate* my mass-market stuff, and fans who dig my mass-market stuff *hate* my hardcore stuff; in fact, most of my mass-market fans aren't even aware of my hardcore double-life."

Hot on the heels of Edward Lee's emergence as a purveyor of extreme horror, another wave of writers came along. Heavily influenced by the original core members of the splat pack, as well as Jack Ketchum, Richard Laymon, and Edward Lee, this group of younger writers—Brian Keene, Bryan Smith, Weston Ochse, Ryan Harding, Wrath James White, Monica J. O'Rourke, Geoff Cooper—drew on these wide array of influences and staked out their own turf in the field. "In the case of Richard Laymon and Jack Ketchum," Brian Keene tells me, "as well as the Splatterpunks and Lansdale, Herbert, and Masterton and a few others, their stuff pushed the boundaries of that time. You know the old Spinal Tap joke about the amps going up to eleven? The first time I read *The Cellar* and *Animals* and *The Girl Next Door* and *The Drive-In*, it was like that—horror fiction cranked up to eleven. And it wasn't just the fiction. The whole Splatterpunk persona really appealed to me as well, early on. Before that, writers were these guys in... not necessarily tweed jackets and pipes, but stuffy, all the same, you know? Then along comes Schow and Skipp & Spector, and they dress like rock stars and *behave* like rock stars. I ate that shit up. That was what I wanted to be when I grew up. Then there's Laymon and Ketchum and Lee thumbing their nose at all rules and standards. Yeah, my course was set. Early on, I wanted to combine the elements of both Splatterpunk and Extreme Horror. And that's what I did."

Unlike Smith and Keene, Wrath James White was not initially influenced by the splatterpunks. "When I began publishing my work in late 1999, early 2000, I had not read a horror novel in nearly a decade. The first modern day horror novel I read was Poppy Z. Brite's *Exquisite Corpse*. I was blown away by that novel. It was as no-holds-barred as the music and movies that were coming out at that time. The next horror novel I read was Brett Easton Ellis's *American Psycho*. To me, those novels seemed like a natural progression from what Stephen King and Clive Barker were doing in the eighties. They mirrored the violence and sexuality of the time. I assumed that they were representative of the current trend in the genre. I had no idea that I was writing anything different from what everyone else was doing. It wasn't until I started getting emails from people who had read my work, calling it 'extreme' that I realized that I was outside the mainstream."

There's no doubt that the splatterpunks of yore had a tremendous influence on writers like White, Smith and Keene. What's interesting now is hearing their thoughts on the new crop of writers coming up in the field who are influenced by *them*. Wrath James White says, "I think the difference between what some of the newer writers who are trying their hand at extreme horror today, and what we were doing back in 2000 is that they are trying to be extreme rather than just trying to tell a good story. There's a difference between telling a story regardless of any taboos, and writing a story for the sole purpose of *breaking* taboos. I should know. I've done both. And I think readers can tell the difference."

Indeed they can. Despite its gag-inducing scenes of revolting violence and perversity, Edward Lee's *The Bighead* and

The Pig are really hardboiled crime pieces. The grotesque nature of their narratives is a natural, organic outgrowth of both tales' plot. Compare Edward Lee's work with that of a novel like *Snuff* by Eric Enck and Adam Huber and its obvious which author actually has a story to tell and which one is simply trying to be shocking for the sake of being shocking. This begs the question: who gets blamed for influencing shoddy work produced by inferior writers trying to cash in on the extreme horror movement?

"What gets the blame?" Brian Keene asks. "How about the person who wrote the work? That seems fair to me. You can't blame us, or Lee or Skipp and Spector. That would be like blaming Stephen King and Dean Koontz for William W. Johnstone and Ruby Jean Jensen."

On the other hand, there is some worthy material being published today that pushes the boundaries and is well written and thought provoking. What's interesting is where the influence is coming from: the splatterpunks of the 1980's or the more modern purveyors of extreme horror like Edward Lee? "I think it's a combination of the two," Brian Keene says. "You look at the work of Wrath James White or Bryan Smith— they have Laymon and Ketchum's cutthroat storytelling style, but the political and social sensibilities and commentary of the best of the splatterpunk era. They're certainly extreme, but they're also subversive. I think it's a wonderful combination."

Extreme horror has been around for over two centuries in various forms. Its use as a device in literature has waxed and waned with the changing of the times. From the works of M. G. Lewis and the Marquis de Sade, to the Grand Guignol theatre in France and the "raw heads and bloody bones" horror fiction in the late Victorian era, to the shudder pulps of the 1930's, to the British Nasties and the splatterpunk movement in the 1980's, to Edward Lee and Richard Laymon, to Brian Keene and Bryan Smith, it is evident that extreme elements in horror fiction have consistently been present. What shocked and disgusted readers of the 1930's shudder pulps may not provoke the same reaction with modern readers used to the extremes found in the work of Wrath James White. However, when taken into context with the sensibilities of those times, and by comparing the works published in the shudder pulps with the more contemporary works that found print in pulps like *Weird Tales*, one can draw a parallel with what is going on today with small presses like Necro Publications versus the more mainstream and critically acclaimed work being published by Subterranean Press or CD Publications.

As to what the future holds for Extreme horror, the jury is out, as it always is. Art is subjective and always has been. The "raw heads and bloody bones" work of Dick Donovan and Clive Pemberton were dismissed by critics and writers of the late Victorian age as nihilistic and violent. For years, the work of Arthur J. Burks and John H. Knox was relatively obscure due to the bulk of their work appearing in the shudder pulps, which was forever tarnished by the intelligentsia of the horror genre. The work of John Skipp and Craig Spector was criticized for its unflinching depiction of sex and violence in the 1980's, as was the early extreme horror of Edward Lee. However, despite all this, they found steady readership during their respective years of activity, and in the case of the splatterpunk and extreme horror era, their work was recognized quicker by legitimate critics of the genre as being seminal in the field (despite comments by those who feel the exact opposite). While these merits can be debated endlessly, only the passing of time will tell if the work of Edward Lee, Wrath James White, or even Skipp & Spector or Richard Laymon will be canonized as classics of horror fiction. It is my belief that they will, and that the works of their less-talented imitators will fade to obscurity.

How much more extreme can things get in horror fiction? One might very well ask how much more extreme can life get? In today's society of being able to watch real executions on Youtube, the proliferation of child pornography and other atrocities on the internet, writers of horror fiction are simply mining what is out there for their work. What was acceptable thirty years ago has become tame by contemporary standards. Yet, despite this, tales of extreme horror written and published even thirty years ago still manages to invoke harsh reactions from even today's most jaded readers. Mendal W. Johnson's *Let's Go Play at the Adams'*, published in 1974, still manages to outrage readers today. Clive Barker's "Pig Blood Blues" and David J. Schow's "Blood Rape of the Lust Ghouls" still gross out today's devotees of Edward Lee and Wrath James White. John Skipp and Craig Spector's *The Cleanup* still manages to provoke hostile reactions from modern readers. "There will always be somebody," says Craig Spector, "some writer who is just a bit more bent than everybody else, more of a mutant. They'll tap right into what is going on, and what comes out will just be that much more warped. It's like I said before, John and I wrote depraved fiction for depraved times. Things are much more depraved now, and it's no wonder that writers who were influenced by us and that came of age within the last decade are turning out stuff that is even more depraved than what John and I and Schow ever came up with. Depraved fiction for depraved times."

Depraved times, indeed. And it's only going to continue to evolve this way.

There are no limits.

Splatterpunk
Recommended
Reading List

W hat follows is a comprehensive list of novels, short story collections, and anthologies that I consider key in the development and canon of extreme horror fiction. My thanks to Bob Strauss for his help in compiling it. This is not an attempt to list every work that falls in this category, but merely a rough sampling of what we feel is the best, and most influential work that pushes the limits of horror fiction. Works are listed in chronological order of composition rather than alphabetical order by author; the Midnight House collections of Clive Pemberton and Dick Donovan are more easily obtainable on the secondary market than their original releases, and contain a far more retrospective selection of their best material from their respective time period (late Victorian era). Most of the books listed here are pretty easily obtainable, albeit some may be pricy ($100 or so for some items). Happy hunting!

In The Beginning

- 120 Days of Sodom – Marquis de Sade
- Justine – Marquis de Sade
- The Monk – Matthew Gregory Lewis

Victorian-Era Splatter

- The Weird O' It – Clive Pemberton (Midnight House)
- The Monster Maker – W. C. Morrow (Midnight House)

Tales From The Splatterpulps

- Murgunstrumm & Others – Hugh B. Cave
- Death Stalks the Night – Hugh B. Cave
- Reunion in Hell – John H. Knox
- The Weird Menace Pulps – ed. Sheldon Jaffrey
- The Opener of the Way – Robert Bloch (easily obtained in the compendium volume *The New Fear*, Fedogan & Bremer, 1994, which also includes Bloch's second Arkham House collection *Pleasant Dreams*)
- The Tongueless Horror – Wyatt Blassingame

The Lost Years

- Johnny Got His Gun – Dalton Trumbo
- Echo of a Curse – R.R. Ryan
- House of Flesh – Bruno Fischer
- I Am Legend – Richard Matheson
- Some of Your Blood – Theodore Sturgeon
- A Clockwork Orange – Anthony Burgess
- The Naked Lunch – William S. Burroughs
- The Harlem Horror – Sir Charles Birkin

- Tales from the Crypt/The Vault of Horror/The Haunt of Fear

Mutants Emerging

- Deliverance – James Dickey
- First Blood – David Morrell
- Shoot – Douglas Fairbairn
- Let's Go Play at the Adams' – Mendal W. Johnson
- The Rats – James Herbert
- Came a Spider – Edward Levy
- The Beast Within – Edward Levy
- Lair – James Herbert
- Baal – Robert R. McCammon
- Satan's Love Child – Brian McNaughton
- The Poacher – Brian McNaughton

A Move Toward The Hardcore

- Off Season – Jack Ketchum
- The Cellar – Richard Laymon
- Cellars – John Shirley
- Son of the Endless Night – John Farris
- The Books of Blood – I – IV – Clive Barker
- The Damnation Game – Clive Barker
- That Hellbound Heart – Clive Barker
- Headhunter – Michael Slade

The Splatterpunk Era

- The Light at the End – John Skipp & Craig Spector
- The Cleanup – John Skipp & Craig Spector
- The Scream – John Skipp & Craig Spector
- Silver Scream, ed. David J. Schow

- Seeing Red – David J. Schow
- The Shaft – David J. Schow
- By Bizarre Hands – Joe R. Lansdale
- The Nightrunners – Joe R. Lansdale
- Darklings – Ray Garton
- Live Girls – Ray Garton
- Crucifax Autumn – Ray Garton
- Scars – Richard Christian Matheson
- Ghoul – Michael Slade
- Flesh – Richard Laymon
- Funland – Richard Laymon
- The Girl Next Door – Jack Ketchum
- Book of the Dead – ed. John Skipp & Craig Spector
- Splatterpunks – ed. Paul Sammon
- American Psycho – Brett Easton Ellis

Post Splatterpunk

- The Pond – Simon Lawrence (R. Karl Largeant)
- The Bridge – John Skipp & Craig Spector
- Animals – John Skipp & Craig Spector
- Book of the Dead 2: Still Dead – ed. John Skipp & Craig Spector
- Close to the Bone- Lucy Taylor
- Created By – Richard Christian Matheson
- The Safety of Unknown Cities – Lucy Taylor
- Ghouls – Edward Lee
- Succubi – Edward Lee
- Splatterpunks II – ed. Paul M. Sammon
- Zombie – Joyce Carol Oates
- The End of Alice – A.M. Homes
- Wetbones – John Shirley

- Really, Really, Really, Really Weird Stories – John Shirley
- In the Mirror of Night – Roberta Lannes
- The Convulsion Factory – Brian Hodge
- Lies and Ugliness – Brian Hodge
- Lost Souls – Poppy Z. Brite
- Exquisite Corpse – Poppy Z. Brite
- The Revelation – Bentley Little
- The Summoning – Bentley Little

Extreme Horror

- Header – Edward Lee
- This Symbiotic Fashion – Charlee Jacob
- Haunter – Charlee Jacob
- The Bighead – Edward Lee
- Goon – Edward Lee & John Pelan
- Shifters – Edward Lee & John Pelan
- Family Tradition – Edward Lee & John Pelan
- Darkside: Horror for the Next Millennium – ed. John Pelan
- Ladies Night – Jack Ketchum
- Right to Life – Jack Ketchum

Extreme Horror For Extreme Times— Modern Day Hardcore

- The Rising – Brian Keene
- City of the Dead – Brian Keene
- Dead Sea – Brian Keene
- Entombed – Brian Keene
- Urban Gothic – Brian Keene
- Blood Crazy – Simon Clark
- Survivor – J. F. Gonzalez

- Fetish – J. F. Gonzalez
- Clickers – J. F. Gonzalez & Mark Williams
- Clickers II – J. F. Gonzalez & Brian Keene
- The Preserve – Patrick Lestewka
- Partners in Chyme – Edward Lee & Ryan Harding
- The Teratologist – Edward Lee & Wrath James White
- Succulent Prey – Wrath James White
- The Resurrectionist – Wrath James White
- The Ruins – Scott Smith
- The Killing Kind – Bryan Smith
- Depraved – Bryan Smith
- Deathbringer – Bryan Smith
- Suffer the Flesh – Monica J. O'Rourke
- Poisoning Eros – Monica J. O'Rourke & Wrath James White
- Genital Grinder – Ryan Harding
- Retribution Inc. – Geoff Cooper
- Answers of Silence – Geoff Cooper

Through a Noir, Darkly

What, exactly, makes a story or novel, noir? First, some history: noir fiction evolved from the hardboiled detective genre which was popularized by pulp magazines like *Dime Detective, Black Mask*, and the pulp that started it all *Detective Story Magazine*. One of the best known stories of the hardboiled detective genre, *The Maltese Falcon* by Dashiell Hammet, first appeared in serialized form in *Black Mask* in the 1920s. Raymond Chandler, Cornell Woolrich, Erle Stanley Gardner, Hugh B. Cave, and Steve Fisher also appeared in the pages of *Black Mask*. All wrote traditional mysteries and crime fiction and had a hand in shaping hardboiled detective fiction.

The 'hardboiled' in hardboiled fiction was originally coined to describe a character who was tough—as in, "that mug's as tough as a hardboiled egg". The physical and mental toughness of characters like Hammett's Sam Spade harken back to a series of stories by Gordon Young that appeared in *Adventure* magazine as early as 1917. Hardboiled detective fiction protagonists are tough-guy detectives that solve mysteries and often confront violence on a regular basis, which often lead to the character feeling burned out and cynical toward their emotions and the world at general.

In hardboiled detective fiction, you always know that the protagonist is somebody to root for. They exude moral integrity; they are the typical good-guys. Noir fiction turns the good guy standard on its head. The protagonist is often a loser, or a misfit, the polar opposite of a good-guys. He is the anti-hero. The noir guy has usually done something that should have killed him or, at the very least, put him in prison for a very long time. He's escaped those outcomes, but is left with a darkness of soul, which puts the "noir" in noir fiction.

It's no coincidence that noir fiction began appearing in the 1930's pulp magazines during the same period that Dillinger and Bonnie & Clyde were in all the newspapers. The Great Depression flipped America upside down. Businessmen weren't the upstanding citizens we thought they were, and bank robbers became heroes. The old standards had failed. Find your own justice. Quite often, in life and in fiction, peoples' actions led them into a downward spiral. Sometimes they didn't make it out alive.

The form blossomed in the 1940's and 1950's, and is probably best exemplified by the works of Jim Thompson, especially his 1951 novel *The Killer Inside Me* (filmed twice, in 1977 with Stacy Keach, and most recently in 2010). Thompson's sordid tale of a small town deputy sheriff who lives a double life as a depraved sociopath strikes a nerve even today. Other writers who helped shape and pioneer noir fiction include James M. Cain (considered a pioneer of noir—his novel *The Postman Always Rings Twice* has also been twice filmed), David Goodis, Charles Williams, Elmore Leonard, Patricia Highsmith, Dorothy B. Hughes, and San Felice (a pseudonym for Margaret Millar, who was married to Kenneth Millar who is known by crime fiction fans as Ross Macdonald).

One thing to note—in the 1930's, while the overwhelming majority of writers who penned hardboiled crime and noir fiction in the pulps were men, there is a good possibility women were responsible for some this material, and it was all written under male pen names. While she didn't write noir fiction per se, a good example of this is Mary Dale Buckner, who wrote under the pseudonym Donald Dale. Buckner wrote violent, over-the-top horror stories exclusively for the weird-menace pulp magazines in the 1930's (*Terror Tales, Horror Stories, Dime Mystery Magazine*).

While the term *Film Noir* is French in origin, the form itself sprang from noir fiction when several well-known novels were adapted into films in the 1940's and 1950's (one of the most well-known being an adaptation of Hammett's *The Maltese Falcon*, with Humphrey Bogart playing Sam Spade). Film noir produced during this era is usually associated with a black and white visual style reminiscent of the German Expressionist period (1913–1931). Story-wise, classic film noir are derived from the hardboiled detective and noir fiction that was prevalent on the magazine and paperback racks of that time.

Noir fiction is still being written and published today. The work of Tom Piccirilli is an excellent example of this form. Most recently, the Hard Case Crime imprint (originally pubished by Dorchester, now by Titan Books) did an excellent job in reprinting lost classics from the 1950's and 1960's, including Steve Fisher, Charles Williams, Cornell Woolrich, and Robert Bloch. Occasionally, new, original noir fiction was published by the imprint—good examples of this were Gun Work by David J. Schow, and Money Shot by Christa Faust. Other current writers of noir fiction include Ed Gorman,

Lawrence Block, Andrew Vachss, Joe R. Lansdale, Megan Abbot, Tana French, and Max Allan Collins. There's also no denying noir fiction's influence contemporary video realm. TV dramas like *Breaking Bad*, as well as most of Quentin Tarantino's career, owe much to classic noirish pulp fiction.

Vampires
In Horror Fiction

One of the most popular archetypes in horror fiction is the vampire. The vampire represents ageless evil, immortality, sexuality, and much more. Of all the icons in horror fiction, the vampire is the most popular.

Vampire lore has existed for ages, and every culture has them. Vampires made their first appearance in horror fiction in "The White Devil" by John Webster way back in 1612. John William Polidori wrote what is considered to be the very first vampire story in 1819 called "The Vampyre". Vampires hit the mainstream in 1845 with the publication of a Penny Dreadful called 'Varney the Vampire' by James Rymer. Published as a serial, this tale of gore, romance, and mystery can almost be seen as a Victorian soap-opera (remember Dark Shadows?). It certainly proved to be popular in its day, and 19th century readers waited eagerly to read each installment. J. Sheridan Le Fanu's 'Carmilla' brought full-blooded homo-sexual themes into vampire fiction for the first time (it's subtle, but there if you read closely) in 1871. It was also the first vampire story to feature the vampire as a three-dimensional, sympathetic character, with human emotions and feelings. In 1897 an Irish lad by the name of Bram Stoker published *Dracula*, which has proven to be one of the most popular and most influential vampire novels of all time.

For the next sixty years vampires featured in horror fiction were firmly in the traditional mold, but there were some pleasant surprises. Hugh B. Cave's short novel "Murgunstrumm," published in 1933, was noted for its gore, fast pace, and a roadside inn crawling with vampires. C. L. Moore's "Shambleau" blended horror with science fiction in her 1933 tale in which a species of vampire searches the galaxy for fresh prey. But it was the 1954 publication of *I Am Legend* by Richard Matheson that broke the traditional mode for future vampire tales. This slim novel chronicled the last man on earth's struggle in a world that has been taken over by vampires. In Dan Simmon's *Carrion Comfort*, the vampires don't live on human blood, they feed on human emotions. Boundaries are stretched even further in Brian Lumley's long running Necroscope series.

Stephen King's *'Salem's Lot* dragged the traditional vampire myth out of the crypt kicking and screaming into the modern world, and a flood of imitators followed, updating the Stoker myth with a mix of success. Standouts in this vein include Robert R. McCammon's *They Thirst*, in which vampires literally destroy the city of Los Angeles, California, and Ray Garton's *Live Girls*, in which the vampires are female and work at peepshow booths.

The most influential and most read author of vampire-oriented fiction at the tail end of this decade is Anne Rice. Publication of her first novel *Interview With a Vampire* in 1976 showed a unique view of the vampire, one that was further developed with *The Vampire Lestat* in 1985. Chelsea Quinn Yarbro, in her novels detailing the exploits of the Vampire

Saint. Germaine, and Rice's further tales of Lestat portray the vampire as a sympathetic figure, an anti-hero with human emotions and their own sense of moral code. This sympathetic appeal, combined with the gothic overtones, has resulted in a wave of vampire fiction that persists to this day.

J. F. Gonzalez's Top 13 Obscure Shockers From The Pulps And Beyond

J. F. Gonzalez was born May 8, 1964 and ten years later, almost to the day, he read his very first pulp horror story. It was "Sweets to the Sweet" by Robert Bloch, and he's been hooked on horror ever since. In addition to reading and collecting pulps and pulp related material, he writes it as well. He is the co-author of such novels as Clickers (with Mark Williams) and Clickers II: The Next Wave (with Brian Keene), both literary homage's to those classic 50's hybrid SF/Horror films as well as the kind of story that might have been featured in an issue of Fantastic. His other novels include Shapeshifter, Bully, The Beloved, Survivor, and Hero (co-written with Wrath James White), among others. His short fiction is collected in Old Ghosts and Other Revenants and When the Darkness Falls.

We all know the classic stories of the genre's greatest writers, right? "The Jar" by Ray Bradbury. "The Ash Tree" by M. R. James. "The Dunwich Horror" by H. P. Lovecraft. "The Mangler" by Stephen King. I could go on with a litany of them, all written by established masters of the genre, and so can you. But what of those forgotten gems of yesteryear? The ones written by writers many people have never heard of or, in some cases, have forgotten, many seeing their only (so far) publication in obscure pulps and small press magazines and rarely reprinted?

Here is my list of those forgotten gems by such writers that are guaranteed to provide that obligatory shiver down your spine or that blood-curdling sense of fear that will remain with you long after you read it. My criteria for choosing them was simple: it had to be the type of story that has stuck with me for years after reading it, and it had to have been penned by a writer either known by those hardcore horror bibliophiles like myself or so obscure that even *they'd* never heard of 'em. Oh yeah... and the stories had to be originally published in obscure pulps and small press magazines and either never or rarely reprinted, making them truly obscure horrific gems.

A note about tracking these down: thanks to the internet, you no longer have to haunt the dusty backrooms of used bookstores and flea markets to find copies of the moldering pulps or periodicals these stories originally appeared in the way I did. Some have been reprinted a time or two since their subsequent appearance, while others, to the best of my knowledge, haven't. So. Track them down. Read them. You'll be glad you did.

1. "Claimed" by Francis Stevens from *The Argosy*, March 6–20, 1920

2. "Beyond the Door" by J. Paul Suter, from *Weird Tales*, April 1923

3. "The Copper Bowl" by George Fielding Elliot, from *Weird Tales*, December 1928

4. "They Bite" by Anthony Boucher from *Unknown Worlds*, August 1943

5. "The Man Who Cried 'Wolf'" by Robert Bloch from *Weird Tales*, May 1945

6. "Island of the Hands" by Margaret St. Clair from *Weird Tales*, September 1952

7. "Call Not There Names" by Everil Worrell, from *Weird Tales*, March 1954

8. "The Other Side" by Arthur Porges, from *Fantastic*, Feb 1964

9. "After Nightfall" by David A. Riley, from *Coven 13*. 1969

10. "Screaming to Get Out" by Janet Fox, from *Weirdbook* #12, 1977

11. "Window" by Bob Leman, *F&SF*, from May 1980

12. "Bagman" by William R. Trotter, 1985, from *Night Cry Magazine*, Fall 1985

13. "14 Garden Grove" by Pierre Comtois, 1986, from *The Horror Show*, Winter 1986

Afterword

It's 9 June and I am sitting in a bar in Southern California and thinking about memory

My friend, J.F. Gonzalez was born not far from here and it is here where his love for horror started. That love stretched from the current, small press authors he found in local shops, to the past through the pulps, pamphlets and plays.

This love of horror turned into a love of history turned into a desire to pass that history along, to keep writers who're fading into the shadows of time in the memory of us all.

Because these lists were not about cannon or classics, about fandom or gatekeeping—they were about remembering.

Remembering who came before, about how the fiction and poetry being written now are a part of a long connection from blogs and eZines to magazines and dime novels, to pulps and serials, through the threads of time back to the first storytellers around campfires talking about the monsters in the darkness.

Workin on *Shadows* has been filled with nothing but memory—remembering plans and talks and rants and the future that did not come.

This work is unfinished, and yet still contains so much. So many works and names and history to keep out of the shadows in our memories.

The truth is, it would have always been unfinished. There would always have been more to add, more history from different parts of the world, more writers forging history in the present, more works who's influence can still be felt today, even as their titles fade into shadows.

Keeping the memory of the past active in the present ensures that present will be remembered as it too slides into the past.

So here, at the end of this unfinished work I charge you to help write more chapters, charge you, as Jesus charged so many of us—go, read, learn from the present, learn from the past, find out how they link, those who inspired those who inspired you—remember where we came from, and we are all connected through memory back to those campfire tales.

And then pass along what you have learned.

Jacob Haddon, somewhere off the 405
June 2022

Biography

J.F. Gonzalez (1964 – 2014) was the author of over thirty books (under his own name as well as several pseudonyms such as Angel Garcia, Zack Venable, Gilbert Schloss, and Richard Long), mostly in the horror and thriller genres, including the seminal *Survivor* and the popular *Clickers* series. Gonzalez sometimes collaborated with authors Mark Williams, Brian Keene, Wrath James White, Mike Oliveri, and others. He was also the author of over two hundred and fifty short stories (again under his own name as well as several pseudonyms), several of which were listed as "Recommended Reads" in Ellen Datlow's annual Year's Best Fantasy and Horror anthologies.

Gonzalez published in both the mass-market, trade, and small press formats. In his lifetime, his publishers included Cemetery Dance Publications, Kensington Books, Leisure Books, HarperCollins, Delirium Books, DarkTales Publishing, Bloodletting Press, Thunderstorm Books, and countless others. He was renowned by his peers for his deep and encompassing knowledge of the genre. His non-fiction has been featured in *Lamplight*, *Afraid*, and elsewhere.

Among his editorial credits are the magazines *Phantasm* and *Iniquities* (both co-edited with Buddy Martinez), and the anthologies *Tooth & Claw* (co-edited with Garrett Peck) and

Downward Spiral (edited under Gilbert Schloss pseudonym). He also ran his own small press, Midnight Library, which published a selection of his own works as well as those of Gord Rollo, Wayne Allen Sallee, Victor Heck and others.

Gonzalez made cameo appearances in the movies *Dr. Blood's Cinema Dungeon* and *Fast Zombies Suck*, and had an un-credited scream cameo in the Lovecraftian short film, *The Stall*. He was one of the first horror writers to ever be asked to speak at the Central Intelligence Agency headquarters in Langley, VA. The first book signing he ever did was with Richard Laymon and Bentley Little (one of the latter's few public appearances).

Born in Inglewood, California, Gonzalez spent most of his life on the West Coast, before moving to Central Pennsylvania in the early 2000's, where he resided with his wife and daughter until passing away from complications of cancer on November 10th, 2014.

In 2017, it was announced that the annual Splatterpunk Awards would include a J.F. Gonzalez Award honoring individuals whose contributions have had a memorable impact on the Splatterpunk and Extreme Horror sub-genres.

Works by J.F. Gonzalez

Novels And Novellas:

- Back From The Dead
- Bully
- Clickers (Co-Written With Mark Williams)
- Clickers II (Co-Written With Brian Keene)
- Clickers III (Co-Written With Brian Keene)
- Clickers Vs. Zombies (Co-Written With Brian Keene)
- Clickers Forever (Edited By Brian Keene)
- Conversion
- Do Unto Others
- Fetish
- Final Retreat (Co-Written With Brian Keene)
- Hero (Co-Written With Wrath James White)
- Monsters And Animals (Co-Written With Wrath James White)
- Primitive
- Restore From Backup (Co-Written With Mike Oliveri)
- Retreat
- Secrets
- Shapeshifter
- Sins Of The Father

- Sixty-Five Stirrup Iron Road (Co-Written With Brian Keene, Wrath James White, Edward Lee, Jack Ketchum, Bryan Smith, Nate Southard, Ryan Harding, And Shane Mckenzie)
- Survivor
- The Beloved
- The Corporation
- The Crossroads (Co-Written With Gabino Iglesias)
- The Killings (Co-Written With Wrath James White)
- They

Collections:

- Old Ghosts And Other Revenants
- Screaming To Get Out & Other Wailings Of The Damned
- The Summoning & Other Eldritch Tales
- That's All Folks
- Up Jumped The Devil
- When The Darkness Falls

for the complete bibliography of J.F. Gonzalez, visit jfgonzalez.org

Attributions

The "Shadows in the Attic" series of articles was published in *LampLight Magazine*

- Reprint Anthologies, Volume 1 Issue 1, September 2012
- The Year's Best Horror Stories, Volume 1 Issue 2, December 2012
- From the Stone Age to the Early Victorian Era, in 3,000 Words, Volume 1 Issue 3, March 2013
- On *The Horror Show*, Volume 1 Issue 4, June 2013
- From the Stone Age to the Early Victorian Era, in 3,000 Words Part Two, or Ghosts, Conte Cruel, and more Victorian era Horror Fiction, Volume 2 Issue 1, September 2013
- From the Stone Age to the Early Victorian Era, in 3,000 Words Part Three, or, Late Victorian and Edwardian Ghostly Fiction and Early Pulp Horror, Volume 2 Issue 2, December 2013
- Weird Tales and its Influence, Weird-menace, Early Horror Movies and Radio Shows, Volume 2 Issue 3, March 2014

- Horror in the Late 1930's and 1940's; British Thrillers, Weird Tales Gets a New Editor, Arkham House, and Neglected Horror Writers of the War Years, Volume 2 Issue 4, June 2014
- The Death of Weird Tales, the Rise of Digest-size Science Fiction Pulps, Comics, Playboy and Other Slick Paper Magazines, Richard Matheson, and Charles Beaumont, Volume 3 Issue 1, September 2014

Published Non-Fiction:

- Diary of a Madman #10, Are The Pulps Really Dead?, *Afraid* Issue 17, October 1993
- Why History 101 is Fundamental, HellNotes.com

The following were first published in this collection:

- J. F. Gonzalez's Top 13 Obscure Shockers From The Pulps And Beyond
- No Limits: Exploring The History Of Splatterpunk And Extreme Horror
- Through a Noir, Darkly
- Vampires In Horror Fiction

Author Index

A list of authors and their works mentioned in this Collection

Alexander Laing
  Novels / Novellas:
  • The Cadaver of Gideon
    Wyck

Alexandre Chatrian

Algernon Blackwood
  Novels / Novellas:
  • The Willows

Allison V. Harding

Ambrose Bierce
  Short Stories:
  • An Occurrence at Owl
    Creek Bridge
  • Chickamauga
  • The Middle Toe of the
    Right Foot

Amelia B. Edwards

Andrew Vachss

Ann Radcliffe
  Novels / Novellas:
  • The Mysteries of Udolpho

Anne Rice
  Novels / Novellas:
  • Interview With a Vampire
  • The Vampire Lestat

Anonymous
  Novels / Novellas:
  • The Animated Skeleton

Anthony Boucher
  Short Stories:

• They Bite

Anthony Burgess
  Novels / Novellas:
  • A Clockwork Orange

Anthony M. Rud
  Short Stories:
  • A Square of Canvas
  • Ooze

Arlton Eadie
  Novels / Novellas:
  • The Trail of the Cloven
    Hoof

Arthur C. Clarke

Arthur Conan Doyle

Arthur Machen
  Novels / Novellas:
  • The Hill of Dreams
  Collections:
  • The House of Souls

Arthur Porges
  Short Stories:
  • The Other Side

August Derleth
  Short Stories:
  • Logoda's Heads

Barbara Roden

Barry Pain
  Short Stories:
  • The Undying Thing

Bentley Little
  Novels / Novellas:
  • The Revelation
  • The Summoning
  Short Stories:
  • Runt
  • Witch Woman

Bernard Capes

Bill Pronzini

Bob Leman
  Short Stories:
  • Window

Bram Stoker
  Novels / Novellas:
  • Dracula

Bret Harte

Brett Easton Ellis
  Novels / Novellas:
  • American Psycho

Brian Hodge
  Collections:
  • Lies and Ugliness
  • The Convulsion Factory
  Short Stories:
  • Oasis
  • Phallasies

Brian Keene
  Novels / Novellas:
  • City of the Dead
  • Dead Sea

• Entombed
• The Rising
• Urban Gothic

Brian Lumley

Brian McNaughton
  Novels / Novellas:
  • Satan's Love Child
  • The Poacher

Bruno Fischer
  Novels / Novellas:
  • House of Flesh

Bryan Smith
  Novels / Novellas:
  • Deathbringer
  • Depraved
  • The Killing Kind

C. L. Moore
  Short Stories:
  • Shambleau

C. M. Eddy Jr.
  Short Stories:
  • The Loved Dead

Caitlen R. Kiernan

Carl Jacobi

Carl Stephenson

Charlee Jacob
  Novels / Novellas:
  • Haunter
  • This Symbiotic Fashion

Charles Baudelaire
Collections:
- Les Fleurs du mal

Charles Beaumont

Charles Birkin
Novels / Novellas:
- The Harlem Horror
Short Stories:
- A Lovely Bunch of Coconuts
- Waiting for Trains

Charles Brockden Brown
Novels / Novellas:
- Wieland

Charles Dickens
Short Stories:
- The Signal Man

Charles L. Grant
Short Stories:
- If Damon Comes

Charles Maturin
Novels / Novellas:
- Melmoth the Wanderer

Charles Williams

Charlotte Bronte
Novels / Novellas:
- Jane Eyre

Charlotte Perkins-Gilman
Short Stories:
- The Yellow Wallpaper

Chelsea Quinn Yarbro

Christa Faust
Novels / Novellas:
- Money Shot

Christopher Marlowe
Novels / Novellas:
- The Tragical History of Doctor Faustus

Clara Reeve
Novels / Novellas:
- Old English Baron

Clark Ashton Smith
Collections:
- Out of Space and Time
Short Stories:
- The Return of the Sorcerer

Clive Barker
Novels / Novellas:
- That Hellbound Heart
- The Books of Blood
- The Damnation Game
Short Stories:
- In the Hills, the Cities
- Pig Blood Blues

Clive Pemberton
Novels / Novellas:
- The Weird O' It

Cornell Woolrich
Novels / Novellas:
- Black Alibi
- Night Has a Thousand Eyes

Craig Spector
Novels / Novellas:
- To Bury the Dead
- Underground

Cynthia Asquith
Collections:
- This Mortal Coil

Cyril Tourneur
Novels / Novellas:
- The Revenger's Tragedy

Dalton Trumbo
Novels / Novellas:
- Johnny Got His Gun

Dan Simmons
Novels / Novellas:
- Carrion Comfort

Daniel Defoe
Novels / Novellas:
- Robinson Crusoe

Short Stories:
- The Ghost in All the Rooms
- The Magician

Dante
Novels / Novellas:
- Inferno

Daphne Du Maurier
Novels / Novellas:
- Rebecca

Dashiell Hammet
Novels / Novellas:
- The Maltese Falcon

David A. Riley
Short Stories:
- After Nightfall

David Campton

David Case

David Goodis

David J. Schow
Novels / Novellas:
- Gore Movie (unpublished)
- Gun Work
- The Shaft

Collections:
- Seeing Red
- Silver Scream

Short Stories:
- Blood Rape of the Lust Ghouls
- One For the Horrors
- Red Light
- The Mystery Buff

David Morrell
Novels / Novellas:
- First Blood

David Niall Wilson

Dean Koontz

Dennis Cooper
Novels / Novellas:
• Frisk

Dennis Etchison
Short Stories:
• The Scar

Dick Donovan
Novels / Novellas:
• The Cave of Blood
• The Mystic Spell

Donald A. Wollheim
Short Stories:
• Mimic

Donald Dale

Donald R. Burleson

Donald Tyson
Short Stories:
• Cruising

Donald Wandrei

Dorothy B. Hughes

Douglas Fairbairn
Novels / Novellas:
• Shoot

E. C. Tubb

E. F. Benson
Collections:
• The Room in the Tower
Short Stories:
• Caterpillars
• The Room in the Tower

E. H. Visiak
Novels / Novellas:
• Medusa

E. T. A. Hoffman
Short Stories:
• The Sandman

Ed Gorman

Eddy C. Bertin

Edgar Allan Poe
Short Stories:
• The Fall of the House of Usher
• The Masque of the Red Death

Edgar Rice Burroughs
Novels / Novellas:
• The Land That Time Forgot

Edith Nesbit
Short Stories:
• John Charrington's Wedding
• Man-Size in Marble

Edith Wharton
Novels / Novellas:
- Afterward

Edmund Snell

Edward Lee
Novels / Novellas:
- Ever Nat
- Ghouls
- Header
- Succubi
- The Bighead

Short Stories:
- The House
- The Pig

Edward Lee and John Pelan
Novels / Novellas:
- Family Tradition
- Goon
- Shifters
- Splatterspunk: The Micah Hayes Stories

Edward Lee and Ryan Harding
Novels / Novellas:
- Partners in Chyme

Edward Lee and Wrath James White
Novels / Novellas:
- The Teratologist

Edward Levy
Novels / Novellas:
- Came a Spider
- The Beast Within

Edward Lucas White
Short Stories:
- Lukundoo
- The House of the Nightmare

Edward Montague
Novels / Novellas:
- The Demon of Sicily

Elizabeth Hand

Elizabeth Massie

Elmore Leonard

Emile Erckmann

Emily Bronte
Novels / Novellas:
- Wuthering Heights

Erckmann-Chatrian
Collections:
- The Man-Wolf and Other Tales

Short Stories:
- The Murderer's Violin
- The Queen of the Bees

Eric Frank Russell

Erle Stanley Gardner

Ernest Hemingway

Evangeline Walton
Novels / Novellas:
- Witch House

Everil Worrell
  Short Stories:
  • Call Not There Names

F. Paul Wilson

F. Scott Fitzgerald

Fitz James O'Brien
  Short Stories:
  • The Child Who Loved a
    Grave
  • The Diamond Lens
  • The Lost Room
  • What Was It?—A Mystery

Flannery O'Conner
  Short Stories:
  • Good Country People

Francis Lathom
  Novels / Novellas:
  • The Midnight Bell

Francis Stevens
  Novels / Novellas:
  • Claimed
  • The Citadel of Fear
  • The Heads of Cerebus
  • The Labyrinth

  Short Stories:
  • The Nightmare
  • Unseen—Unfeared

Frank Belknap Long
  Collections:
  • The Hounds of Tindalos

Short Stories:
• The Space Eaters

Frank Norris

Franz Kafka
  Novels / Novellas:
  • The Trial

Frederick C. Davis
  Short Stories:
  • The Molemen Want Your
    Eyes

Fredric Brown
  Novels / Novellas:
  • The Screaming Mimi

Fritz Leiber
  Novels / Novellas:
  • Conjure Wife

  Collections:
  • Night's Black Agents

  Short Stories:
  • Diary in the Snow
  • Mr. Bauer and the Atoms
  • Smoke Ghost
  • The Hill and the Hole
  • The Hound

G. K. Chesterton
  Novels / Novellas:
  • The Man Who Was
    Thursday

G. Wayne Miller

Garnett Radcliff

Gary L. Raisor

Geoff Cooper
Novels / Novellas:
- Retribution Inc.
Collections:
- Answers of Silence

George Brewer
Novels / Novellas:
- The Witch of
  Ravensworth

George Fielding Eliot
Short Stories:
- The Copper Bowl

George R. R. Martin
Short Stories:
- Sandkings

George W. M. Reynolds

Gerald Durrell
Short Stories:
- The Entrance

Gerald Kersh
Novels / Novellas:
- Night and the City
Short Stories:
- Men Without Bones

Gerard Houarner

Gertrude Atherton

Gordon Young

Graham Masterton
Short Stories:
- Eric the Pie

Greye La Spina
Novels / Novellas:
- Invaders From the Dark
- Wolf of the Steppes

Guy de Maupassant
Short Stories:
- The Horla

Guy N. Smith

H. B. Gregory
Novels / Novellas:
- Dark Sanctuary

H. Bedford Jones

H. F. Arnold
Short Stories:
- The Night Wire

H. G. Wells
Novels / Novellas:
- The Island of Doctor
  Moreau
- The War of the Worlds

H. P. Lovecraft
Novels / Novellas:
- At the Mountains of
  Madness
Collections:
- Beyond the Wall of Sleep
- Tales of the Cthulhu
  Mythos
- The Best of H. P.
  Lovecraft
- The Outsider and Others
Short Stories:
- Pickman's Model
- The Call of Cthulhu
- The Color Out of Space
- The Dunwich Horror
- The Festival
- The Nameless City
- The Outsider

H. Russell Wakefield
Collections:
- The Clock Strikes Twelve

Hanns Heinz Ewers
Novels / Novellas:
- Alraune
- Der Zauberlehrling
Short Stories:
- The Spider

Harlan Ellison

Harold Lawlor

Harriet Prescott Spofford

Harry Adam Knight

Henry James
Novels / Novellas:
- The Turn of the Screw

Henry Kuttner

Henry S. Whitehead
Collections:
- Jumbee and Other
  Uncanny Tales
- West India Lights
Short Stories:
- Cassius

Herman Melville
Novels / Novellas:
- Moby Dick
- The Confidence Man
Short Stories:
- Bartleby the Scrivener

Homer
Novels / Novellas:
- The Iliad
- The Odyssey

Honore de Balzac
Short Stories:
- La Grande Breteche

Horace Walpole
Novels / Novellas:
- The Castle of Otranto

Hugh B. Cave
Collections:
- Death Stalks the Night
- Murgunstrumm & Others

Short Stories:
- Murgunstrumm

Ira Levin
Novels / Novellas:
- Rosemary's Baby

Isak Dinesan
Short Stories:
- The Sailor-Boy's Tale

J. F. Gonzalez
Novels / Novellas:
- Bully
- Fetish
- Hero
- Shapeshifter
- Survivor
- The Beloved

Collections:
- Old Ghosts and Other Revenants
- When the Darkness Falls

Short Stories:
- The Wrong Guy

J. F. Gonzalez and Brian Keene
Novels / Novellas:
- Clickers II

J. F. Gonzalez and Mark Williams
Novels / Novellas:
- Clickers

J. K. Huysmans

J. N. Williamson

J. Paul Suter
Short Stories:
- Beyond the Door

Jack Finney
Novels / Novellas:
- The Body Snatchers

Jack Ketchum
Novels / Novellas:
- Ladies Night
- Off Season
- Right to Life
- The Girl Next Door

Jack London
Short Stories:
- A Thousand Deaths

Jack Snow

Jack Sullivan

Jack Williamson
Novels / Novellas:
- Darker Than You Think

Short Stories:
- Wolves of Darkness

James Dickey
Novels / Novellas:
- Deliverance

James Herbert
Novels / Novellas:
- Lair
- Moon
- Shrine
- The Fog
- The Rats

James Hogg
Novels / Novellas:
- The Confessions of a
  Justified Sinner

James M. Cain
Novels / Novellas:
- The Postman Always
  Rings Twice

James Malcom Rymer
Novels / Novellas:
- A String of Pearls
- Varney the Vampire

Jane Austen
Novels / Novellas:
- Northanger Abbey

Jane Rice
Short Stories:
- The Idol of the Flies

Janet Fox
Short Stories:
- Screaming to Get Out

Jean Ray
Short Stories:
- The Shadowy Street

Jeremias Gotthelf
Novels / Novellas:
- The Black Spider

Jerome Bixby
Short Stories:
- It's a Good Life!

Jesse Douglas Kerruish
Novels / Novellas:
- The Undying Monster

Jim Thompson
Novels / Novellas:
- The Killer Inside Me

Joe R. Lansdale
Novels / Novellas:
- The Nightrunners
Collections:
- By Bizarre Hands
Short Stories:
- God of the Razor
- My Dead Dog, Bobby
- The Fat Man
- The Shaggy House

John Brunner

John Buchan

John Collier
Short Stories:
- Thus I Refute Beelzy

John Coyne

John Farris
Novels / Novellas:
• Son of the Endless Night

John H. Knox
Collections:
• Reunion in Hell

John Metcalfe
Collections:
• The Smoking Leg and
Other Stories

John Shirley
Novels / Novellas:
• Cellars
• Wetbones
Collections:
• Really, Really, Really,
Really Weird Stories

John Skipp
Short Stories:
• Film At Eleven

John Skipp and Cody Goodfellow
Novels / Novellas:
• Jake's Wake

John Skipp and Craig Spector
Novels / Novellas:
• Animals
• The Bridge
• The Cleanup
• The Light at the End

• The Scream
Short Stories:
• Company

John Skipp and Marc Levinthal
Novels / Novellas:
• The Emerald Burrito of
Oz

John W. Campbell
Short Stories:
• Who Goes There?

John Webster
Novels / Novellas:
• The White Devil

John William Polidori
Short Stories:
• The Vampyre

Jonathan Swift
Novels / Novellas:
• Gulliver's Travels

Joseph Conrad
Novels / Novellas:
• The Heart of Darkness

Joseph Payne Brennan
Short Stories:
• Slime

Joseph Sheridan Le Fanu
Novels / Novellas:
• Carmilla
• Green Tea
• Uncle Silas

Joyce Carol Oates
Novels / Novellas:
- Zombie

Short Stories:
- A Good Man is Hard to Find
- Nightside

Karl Edward Wagner
Novels / Novellas:
- Gods in Darkness
- In a Lonely Place

Short Stories:
- Sticks

Kathe Koja

Kelley Armstrong
Short Stories:
- A Haunted House of Her Own

Kevin J. Anderson

Kit Reed

L. A. Lewis
Short Stories:
- The Tower of Moab

L. P. Hartley

L. Ron Hubbard
Novels / Novellas:
- Fear
- Typewriter in the Sky

Lawrence Block

Lawrence C. Connolly
Short Stories:
- Echoes
- Mrs. Halfbooger's Basement

Leonard Cline
Novels / Novellas:
- The Dark Chamber

Lorenz Flammenberg
Novels / Novellas:
- The Necromancer; or, The Tale of the Black Forest

Lucy Clifford
Short Stories:
- The New Mother

Lucy Taylor
Novels / Novellas:
- The Safety of Unknown Cities

Collections:
- Close to the Bone
- The Flesh Artist

Luigi Ugolini
Short Stories:
- The Vegetable Man

M. P. Shiel
Novels / Novellas:
- The Purple Cloud

M. R. James
Collections:
- A Pleasing Terror
- Ghost Stories of an Antiquary

Short Stories:
- Canon Albert's Scrapbook
- Lost Hearts
- Oh Whistle and I'll Come to You, My Lad
- The Ash Tree

Manly Wade Wellman
Short Stories:
- For Fear of Little Men

Margaret Millar

Margaret Oliphant

Margaret St. Clair
Short Stories:
- Island of the Hands

Marie Belloc Lowndes
Novels / Novellas:
- The Lodger

Mark A. Parks

Mark Hansom

Mark Twain

Mark Williams

Marquis de Sade
Novels / Novellas:
- 120 Days of Sodom
- Justine

Mary Anne Radliffe
Novels / Novellas:
- Manfrone

Mary Dale Buckner

Mary Danby

Mary Elizabeth Braddon

Mary Elizabeth Counselman
Short Stories:
- The Three Marked Pennies

Mary Shelly
Novels / Novellas:
- Frankenstein

Mary Wilkins-Freeman
Collections:
- The Wind in the Rose Bush and Other Stories of the Supernatural

Short Stories:
- Luella Miller
- The Shadows on the Wall

Matthew Gregory Lewis
Novels / Novellas:
- The Monk

Maurice Level
Short Stories:
- In the Light of the Red Lamp

Max Allan Collins

Megan Abbot

Mendal W. Johnson
Novels / Novellas:
- Let's Go Play at the
  Adams

Michael Shea
Short Stories:
- The Autopsy

Michael Slade
Novels / Novellas:
- Ghoul
- Headhunter

Michel Bernanos
Novels / Novellas:
- The Other Side of the
  Mountain

Monica J. O'Rourke
Novels / Novellas:
- Suffer the Flesh

Monica J. O'Rourke and Wrath
James White
Novels / Novellas:
- Poisoning Eros

Mrs. J. H. Riddell

Murray Leinster

Nathanael West
Novels / Novellas:
- Day of the Locust
- Miss Lonelyhearts

Nathaniel Hawthorne
Novels / Novellas:
- The House of the Seven
  Gables

Short Stories:
- Ethan Brand
- Rappacini's Daughter
- Young Goodman Brown

Oscar Wilde
Novels / Novellas:
- The Picture of Dorian
  Gray

Otis Adelbert Kline

Patricia Highsmith

Patrick Lestewka
Novels / Novellas:
- The Preserve

Paul Bailey
Novels / Novellas:
- Deliver Me From Eva

Peter Haining

Peter Straub

Pierre Comtois
Short Stories:
- 14 Garden Grove

Poppy Z. Brite
Novels / Novellas:
- Exquisite Corpse

Short Stories:

- A Taste of Blood and Altars

R. Murray Gilchrist

Short Stories:
- The Lover's Ordeal

R. R. Ryan

Novels / Novellas:
- Echo of a Curse
- Freak Museum
- The Subjugated Beast

Ramsey Campbell

Short Stories:
- Drawing In
- The Companion

Ray Bradbury

Novels / Novellas:
- Fahrenheit 451

Collections:
- Bradbury Stories: 100 of His Most Celebrated Tales
- Dark Carnival
- The Golden Apples of the Sun
- The Illustrated Man
- The October Country
- The Stories of Ray Bradbury

Short Stories:
- The Crowd
- The Jar
- The Scythe
- The Small Assassin
- The Smiling People

Ray Garton

Novels / Novellas:
- Crucifax Autumn
- Darklings
- Live Girls

Raymond Chandler

Reggie Oliver

Richard Christian Matheson

Novels / Novellas:
- Created By

Collections:
- Dystopia
- Scars

Richard Dalby

Richard Laymon

Novels / Novellas:
- Flesh
- Funland
- The Cellar

Short Stories:
- The Grab

Richard Marsh

Novels / Novellas:
- The Beetle

Richard Matheson

Novels / Novellas:
- Fury on Sunday
- I Am Legend
- Someone is Bleeding

Short Stories:
- Born of Man and Woman
- Duel
- Prey

Richard Moore
Short Stories:
- The Devil Behind You

Richard T. Chizmar

Rick Hautala
Novels / Novellas:
- Moondeath
- Night Stone

Collections:
- Bedbugs

Roald Dahl
Short Stories:
- Man From the South

Robert Aickman

Robert Barbor Johnson
Short Stories:
- Far Below

Robert Bloch
Novels / Novellas:
- Psycho

Collections:
- The Early Fears
- The Opener of the Way

Short Stories:
- Lilies
- Mannikins of Horror
- Sweets to the Sweet

- The Animal Fair
- The Feast in the Abbey
- The Man Who Collected Poe
- The Man Who Cried 'Wolf'
- Yours Truly, Jack the Ripper

Robert Browning

Robert Devereaux

Robert E. Howard
Collections:
- Skull-face and Others

Robert G. Anderson

Robert Hugh Benson
Novels / Novellas:
- The Necromancers

Robert Louis Stevenson
Novels / Novellas:
- The Strange Case of Doctor Jekyll and Mr. Hyde
- Treasure Island

Robert R. McCammon
Novels / Novellas:
- Baal
- They Thirst

Robert Sheckly

Robert W. Chambers
Collections:
- The King in Yellow

Short Stories:
- In the Court of the Dragon
- The Mask
- The Repairer of Reputations
- The Yellow Sign

Robert Weinberg

Roberta Lannes
Novels / Novellas:
- In the Mirror of Night

Rudyard Kipling

Russell Kirk

Ryan Harding
Collections:
- Genital Grinder

Ryunosuke Akutagawa
Short Stories:
- The Hell Screen

Saki

Scott Smith
Novels / Novellas:
- The Ruins

Seabury Quinn

Shaun Hutson

Shirley Jackson
Short Stories:
- The Lottery

Simon Clark
Short Stories:
- ...Beside the Seaside, Beside the Sea

Simon Lawrence
Novels / Novellas:
- The Pond

Stefan Grabinski

Stephen Crane
Short Stories:
- Manacled

Stephen King
Novels / Novellas:
- 'Salem's Lot
- Carrie

Short Stories:
- Crouch End
- Gray Matter
- The Man in the Black Suit
- The Mangler
- The Raft

Steve Fisher

Steve Rasnic Tem
Short Stories:
- Self-Possessed

Susan Hill

Susan M. Watkins

T. E. D. Klein
Short Stories:

Wilkie Collins

William Beckford
   Novels / Novellas:
    • Vathek

William F. Nolan

William Faulkner

William Hope Hodgson
   Novels / Novellas:
    • The Boats of the "Glen
      Carrig"
    • The House on the
      Borderland
   Short Stories:
    • Out of the Storm
    • The Gateway of the
      Monster
    • The Mystery of the
      Derelict
    • The Voice in the Night

William Peter Blatty
   Novels / Novellas:
    • The Exorcist

William R. Trotter
   Short Stories:
    • Bagman

William S. Burroughs
   Novels / Novellas:
    • The Naked Lunch

William Shakespeare
   Novels / Novellas:
    • Hamlet
    • The Tragedy of Macbeth

William Sloane
   Novels / Novellas:
    • The Edge of Running
      Water

Wrath James White
   Novels / Novellas:
    • Succulent Prey
    • The Resurrectionist

Wyatt Blassingame

Yvonne Navarro

LampLight

Volume One
Edited by Jacob Haddon

LampLight Volume 1

lamplightmagazine.com/volume-1

This 450 page anthology of the first year of LampLight Magazine collects four amazing issues from September 2012 - June 2013.

Features the complete serial novella "And I Watered It With Tears" by Kevin Lucia. Fiction and interviews with Robert Ford, Kelli Owen, Ronald Malfi, and Elizabeth Massie.

J.F. Gonzalez takes us through the history of the genre with his Shadows in the Attic articles. LampLight classics bring you some of those past voices to experience again.

Fiction by William Meikle, Nathan Yocum, Rahul Kanakia, Ian Creasey, Mandy DeGeit, D.J. Cockburn, Christopher Fryer, Christopher Kelly, Tim Lieder, Jamie Lackey, Matthew Warner, Sheri White, Dinos Kellis, S. R. Mastrantone, Mjke Wood, Delbert R. Gardner, Michele Mixell, Sarah Rhett, Armel Dagorn, E. Catherine Tobler

LampLight

Volume Two
Edited by Jacob Haddon

LampLight Volume 2

lamplightmagazine.com/volume-1

This second annual anthology from LampLight Magazine collects the four great issues from September 2013 to June 2014

Includes the complete novella, The Devoted, featuring Jonathan Crowley, by James A Moore.

Fiction and interviews from our featured writers: Norman Prentiss, Kealan Patrick Burke, Mary SanGiovanni and Holly Newstein.

J.F. Gonzalez continues his history of the genre in his Shadows in the Attic series. LampLight Classics brings you some great classic stories.

Fiction by: Michael Knost, Christopher Bleakley, Emma Whitehall, David Tallerman, M. R. Jordan, Lauren Forry, Dave Thomas, Arinn Dembo, Bracken MacLeod, doungjai gam, Tim W Boiteau, Alethea Eason, Lucy A Snyder, Colleen Jurkiewicz, Curtis James McConnell, Victor Cypert, Catherine Grant

Printed by BoD˝in Norderstedt, Germany

9 781088 019566